NON-STATE ACTORS IN ASSET RECOVERY

DANIEL THELESKLAF /
PEDRO GOMES PEREIRA (EDS.)
BASEL INSTITUTE ON GOVERNANCE

NON-STATE ACTORS IN ASSET RECOVERY

PETER LANG
Bern · Berlin · Bruxelles · Frankfurt am Main · New York · Oxford · Wien

Bibliographic information published by die Deutsche Nationalbibliothek
Die Deutsche Nationalbibliothek lists this publication in the Deutsche Nationalbibliografie; detailed bibliographic data is available on the Internet at ‹http://dnb.d-nb.de›.

British Library Cataloguing-in-Publication Data: A catalogue record for this book is available from The British Library, Great Britain

The opinions expressed are solely of the author and do not represent the view of the Basel Institute on Governance.

Cover Design: Eva Rolli, Peter Lang Bern

ISBN 978-3-0343-1073-4

Hochfeldstrasse 32, CH-3012 Bern, Switzerland
info@peterlang.com, www.peterlang.com

Printed in Switzerland

Table of Contents

Preface

This is a timely book. Both 'asset recovery' and 'non-state actors' are relatively new concepts of law and politics. Asset recovery is an activity mandated by Chapter V of the UNCAC which today has 154 parties.[1] Under the relevant provisions, state parties have to trace, freeze and seize proceeds of criminal corruption and to return property to prior legitimate owners. NSAs – tellingly – escape a positive definition. They are actors which are not states. Usually, they are divided into three types: Inter-governmental actors (international organisations, such as the World Bank), non-governmental and non-for profit actors (NGOs), and business actors (including banks and transnational corporations). These three types of actors represent three societal spheres: the governmental sphere, civil society, and the corporate sphere.

The adoption and entry into force of the UNCAC manifests that the international community realised corruption to be one of the most important obstacles to sustainable development and the rule of law.[2] Combating corruption is therefore a high priority of global politics and governance, ultimately in the interest of global peace, the international rule of law, prosperity, and human well-being. In the past years, particularly corrupt regimes have broken down in various regions of the world. The current challenge is, however, to identify, trace, seize, and repatriate stolen money which has often been transferred to well-known financial centres such as Switzerland. The challenge is both practical and legal. It is not sufficient to identify accounts and to lay hands on money in a physical sense, but to respect the technicalities of

1 United Nations Convention against Corruption (UNCAC) of 31 October 2003, entered into force on 14 December 2005, United Nations Treaty Series, vol. 2349, p. 41; UN-Doc. A/58/422.

2 Foreword by Secretary Kofi Annan to the UNCAC 2003: 'Corruption … undermines democracy and the rule of law … is a major obstacle to poverty alleviation and development.' See in this sense also the preamble of GA Res. 58/4 of 31 Oct. 2003 (endorsing UNCAC), and the preamble of UNCAC itself. In scholarship Krista Nadukavukaren Schefer, 'Causation in the Corruption – Human Rights Relationship', *Rechtswissenschaft*, 1 (2010), 397–425.

the mutual legal assistance procedures, a due process, property rights, and possible good faith of the various institutions involved. Asset recovery must, put differently, be effective, legal, and legitimate.

The currently quite bleak progress in asset recovery suggests that the state and purely governmental authorities are not capable of conducting asset recovery processes on their own. So how can NSAs, ranging from inter-governmental bodies over specialised NGOs and the media to the baking sector, contribute to the effectiveness and legitimacy of asset recovery? A key word seems to be information. Most of the contributions of this book highlight the NSAs' particular function of gathering and disseminating information. It is the specialist expertise concerning particular countries, the technicalities of financial transactions, and of legal procedures which the various NSAs furnish. However, the information they possess must also be processed, put together, and used reasonably. If NSAs can, through their contribution, render asset recovery more effective, they might cause legitimacy problems. It is, for example, doubtful whether the monitoring of the spending of money recovered from an ousted dictator by the new government of a developing country can be legitimately entrusted to an NGO which does not enjoy formally democratic credentials.

The contributions in this book raise and explore these and further questions. The volume explores different aspects of the involvement of NSAs in asset recovery processes from different disciplinary perspectives, and the chapters are informed by the diverse practical experience of the contributors. The editors themselves are leaders of the Basel Institute on Governance, an independent, non-for-profit think tank affiliated to the University of Basel, which is, in one of its branches, specialised on asset recovery. Both editors have hands-on experience in asset recovery which guided their choices of topics and contributors. This book seeks not only to spearhead interdisciplinary research on the matter of asset recovery, but also to benefit law and policy makers through the sharing of insider-knowledge, and to inspire legal reform on various aspects of mutual legal assistance. 'Non State Actors in Asset Recovery' is hoped to contribute to making asset recovery a functioning and valuable tool of global governance.

Anne Peters
Professor of Public International and Constitutional Law, Dr. iur., LL.M. (Harvard)
Vice-president of the Board of the Basel Institute on Governance.

September 2011

Non-state actors experts' meeting

The UNCAC is the most comprehensive international instrument to date for the fight against corruption and for the recovery of stolen assets. As a fundamental principle to the Convention, asset recovery is thus a major step for the international community in preventing and combating corruption.

The UNCAC calls for the involvement of civil society in its article 13. The Report on the Experts' meeting of the CoSP, held in November 2009 in Doha, highlighted the role of civil society in the prevention of corruption and applicability of Chapter II (Prevention) of the UNCAC:

'(...) [P]reventive measures set forth by the Convention concerned both the public and the private sectors and underscored the role of other parts of society, such as non-governmental organizations, the media and community-based initiatives. That set of measures constituted recognition that each member of society, individually and collectively, had a contribution to make to a culture of integrity and that preventing and fighting corruption was a shared responsibility.'

'Speakers also stressed the need to encourage the involvement of civil society and the media in preventing corruption at the national level. A number of speakers argued in favour of promoting public-private partnerships to prevent corruption.'

Said report concludes that there are three basic conditions for the successful implementation of the UNCAC: political will, sufficient resources and the active involvement of civil society. Concerning the latter, it is composed of voluntary civic and social organisations and institutions that form the basis of a functioning society as opposed to structures of the state.

On the other hand, NSAs have a much wider definition, which encompasses civil society. NSAs are thus neither states nor intergovernmental organisations: they include, but are not limited to NGOs, the academia, the media, and the private sector that play an important role in the asset recovery process. The role of NSAs in combating corruption is undeniable and their involvement in such as task contained in article 39 of the UNCAC and also in the Annex II of the 2010 Good Practice Guidance on Internal Controls, Ethics, and Compliance, which is an integral part of the OECD Recommendation for Further Combating Bribery of Foreign Public Officials in International Business Transactions of 26 November 2009.

NSAs help generate the impetus for reforms that might otherwise be unpopular with political actors. They are responsible for monitoring and actively reporting state activities, ensuring that the rule of law is upheld, and strengthening democracy, democratic institution and the overall democratic processes. They are also businesses whose activities overlap and converge with the areas that fall under the processes of asset recovery: there are good examples of initiatives of the private sector (e.g., the Wolfsberg Group) that enable higher success rates in the prevention and combating of corruption.

Understanding asset recovery and the asset recovery process is paramount in order to identify the role NSAs are to play a part. Asset recovery requires the interaction of both state and NSAs in order to pursue the most effective policies to address said agenda.

The asset recovery process encompasses procedures that vary from tracing proceeds of corruption, conducting complex financial investigations, mutual legal assistance, seizing of assets – often found in both the victim and recipient jurisdictions of the stolen assets –, confiscation and repatriation. Monitoring of the returned assets may also be considered an additional step. The success of the process also depends of specific knowledge areas that must communicate and intertwine to produce a comprehensive strategy on a case-by-case basis.

The brief overview above shows that the asset recovery process requires a multi-faceted approach and response from the NSAs. On one side, there are financial institutions, which play their part in the process, as the proceeds of crime will make their way – whether voluntarily or involuntarily – through the financial sector. Auditing firms likewise are pivotal to the success of asset recovery initiatives, as external auditing, financial investigation and forensic auditing may show any wrongdoing from the private and public sectors, triggering the appropriate response. Service providers too play an important role, whether providing lists of PEPs or other forms of information and communication technologies (ICTs) to allow for a more efficient control of the flow of information and allow for more effective preventive measures. The legal sector also plays an important role both in the prevention – by providing correct information to their clients, so as to prevent unlawfulness of their actions – and in litigation, by ensuring that the rule of law is upheld and criminals are brought to justice and held accountable for their actions.

On the other side of the spectrum, there are the NGOs, which monitor the state and international initiatives and actions to ensure the democratic processes. They assist in ensuring checks and balances with the asset recovery process. These either act on a policy-making level, or seek a more hands-on approach, often partnering with law firms to litigate for the rights of the victim country. They also play an important role in ensuring greater transparency in monitoring the assets returned to victim countries.

Bearing this in mind, the Basel Institute on Governance (in co-organisation with the IACA) hosted and experts' meeting in September 2010 with NSAs that play an important role in the asset recovery processes. Attendance to the meeting included prominent NSAs from both developing and developed countries that play and important and active role in the asset recovery processes. During the meeting a diverse group of NSAs discussed their experiences and initiatives in the asset recovery process and drew several conclusions on how they could better assist.

I. The non-state actors experts' meeting

The meeting was divided into five main theme groups: academia, civil society, private sector, service providers and media, as each of these groups of NSAs play a specific but equally important role within asset recovery. The meeting sought to clarify the roles of the NSAs in their respective fields, identify potential overlaps, and draw up areas in which these areas could drive the asset recovery agenda in co-ordination.

The participants discussed important themes linked to asset recovery such as the advocacy work by CSOs in recovering stolen assets, the need to conduct thorough research and to collect reliable data in the fields related to asset recovery, as well as the use of civil litigation and PIL in the asset recovery process and the monitoring of returned assets to ensure their appropriate utilisation. The meeting further discussed the role of the financial and insurance industries, and the private sector, in the asset recovery processes. The need to engage in collaborative strategies that take the asset recovery efforts one step further was discussed throughout the experts' meeting by all the theme groups.

Keynote presentation: Andrew Feinstein, Corruption Watch

Mr. Feinstein's presentation focused on NSAs in asset recovery, touching upon corruption and its impact on the victims. Several key asset recovery angles to corporate bribery were mentioned, including the fact that:

- Bribes are often held and paid offshore or in developed countries' banking systems. Identifying and confiscating such bribes, as well as slush funds used to pay bribes, is crucial to fighting corruption.
- There will increasingly be a question of what corporate sanctions should be imposed and how much of the sanction should be paid as reparation to the countries concerned.

Mr. Feinstein mentioned that reparations have recently started to become a feature of plea agreements in the UK with companies admitting guilt to paying bribes in foreign countries. In the first of such cases, a company agreed to pay, in addition to fines, costs and confiscation, reparations to the governments of Jamaica and Ghana.

However, despite admitting to paying bribes in four other countries and confessing to a culture of bribery in the company, the plea agreement was structured in such a way that reparations were paid only to Jamaica and Ghana due to the fact details of the bribes and the names of those who they were paid out to were provided to the English court. Furthermore, Mr. Feinstein pointed out that there was an initial reluctance on the part of the governments of Jamaica and Ghana to accept the reparation payments (GBP 139,000 to Jamaica and GBP 658,000 to Ghana).

Despite of this novel approach in including reparation payments, Mr. Feinstein highlighted that the reparation approach of the SFO was called into question by a high court judge at the end of March 2010 in another bribery case involving a British company. The High Court questioned the authority the SFO had to channel confiscated funds to foreign governments and raised concerns about the money being recycled through corruption.

Mr. Feinstein argued that ensuring that reparations are part of any sanction against companies found guilty of paying bribes is a highly laudable and principled approach, as it focuses public attention to the fact that bribery is a form of theft from developing countries (although whether from the state or its citizens is obviously a contentious point in certain circumstances). It does establish the principle that there is no reason why developed countries that fine the companies involved should be the sole financial beneficiaries of the sanctions on criminal activity whose victims are often in developing countries. However, Mr. Feinstein noted that these reparations seem to be a part of a trade-off with the companies concerned for not pursuing other allegations against them in other countries.

Another issue brought forth by Mr. Feinstein related to the reparation sums. The keynote speaker informed that, in a case involving a company, the reparation sums lead to complaints from citizens in the countries concerned. Mr. Feinstein concluded that, if authorities in the UK, and possibly other jurisdictions, continue to fine companies only a tiny percentage of the profits made on the corrupt deals, the reparations approach might only further antagonize people in the victim countries.

Mr. Feinstein concluded that the reparations approach needs proper international and institutional framework so that (i) there are clear rules and guidelines for how this money should be spent, and (ii) other developed countries prosecuting companies for foreign bribery can follow suit.

Civil society panel

The civil-society panel was comprised of Maud Perdriel-Vaissière of Sherpa (France); Ernest Mpararo, of the *Ligue Congolaise contre la Corruption* – LICOCO (Democratic Republic of Congo); and Max Mader, of the *Aktion Finanzplatz Schweiz* (Switzerland). Gillian Dell, from Transparency International, moderated the panel.

The panel focused on the importance of civil society in the asset recovery process and in AML initiatives through litigation and victim representation. It was pointed out that CSOs are in need for clearer rules on their participation in court proceedings, in order to be able to push cases forward and bring corrupt officials to justice. One of the reasons is the fact that the UNCAC is centred on state actors.

As an example of such initiatives, Ms. Perdriel-Vaissière brought forward the recent case Sherpa and TI France brought to French courts against heads of state of African countries. Ms. Perdriel-Vaissière touched upon the issue that there is currently no clear international framework to ensure access to justice in the recipient state when victim states are unwilling or cannot initiate asset recovery proceedings. Another issue is the fact that in this scenario there may be no safeguards when MLA proceedings fail. For this reason, third party litigation and PIL[1] should be incorporated in the international legal framework to act as a subsidiary measure to ensure access to justice.

Ms. Perdriel-Vaissière explained that Sherpa and two other NGOs filed a legal complaint before the French public prosecutor's office against the ruling families of several African states, alleging they owned millions of Euros worth of properties in France that could not be the fruits of their official salaries. It was argued that the properties would have likely required the use of stolen public assets. The subsequent police investigation confirmed most of the allegations and further uncovered more assets in French territory. Despite the findings,

1 As defined by Black's Law Dictionary, public interest litigation is 'a legal action initiated in a court of law for the enforcement of public interest or general interest in which the public or class of the community have pecuniary interest or some interest by which their legal rights or liabilities are affected.'

the investigation was closed after the Public Prosecution ruled that the crimes were 'insufficiently characterised'.

The plaintiffs then requested the investigating magistrate to resume the investigations that had been closed by the prosecutor. The case is currently pending a decision by the *Cour de Cassation* following the claim by the representatives of an African leader that 'Transparency International had no right to act as plaintiffs against heads of state.' In that regard, Ms. Perdriel-Vaissière raised the argument that, if a CSO which had such a direct link to fighting corruption as TI was not successful in bringing claims, who else would have such capacity? Ms. Perdriel-Vaissière concluded that this is an important question as it is difficult to precise and single out the direct victims of corruption.

The importance of civil society in advocacy and monitoring of returned asset was brought to discussion. Mr. Mpararo discussed this as the main role that civil society is playing in the DRC, and its importance for the cause of asset recovery. Mr. Mpararo mentioned that some of the problematic that civil society is currently facing in the DRC, such as the fact that the donor community is not sponsoring anti-corruption activities in the DRC, and the perception seems to be that they are more concerned with doing business rather that with corruption.

Mr. Mpararo brought forth the challenges faced by civil society in developing countries. One of the elements he touched upon was the fact that the DRC had not yet ratified the UNCAC and that there is currently no internal legislation in place that enables Congolese authorities to recover stolen assets. Thus, Mr. Mpararo envisages that one of the roles that civil society could play in such circumstances would be to push for legal reforms that would enable anti-corruption policies and asset recovery initiatives.

Another challenge that is faced in developing countries includes the lack of capacities in the judiciary, when dealing with the asset recovery processes. Furthermore, Mr. Mpararo indicated an additional challenge, which is the fact that stolen assets seem to be going to more to less conventional jurisdictions such as Dubai, Singapore and China, and less to traditional European jurisdictions, as a consequence to tighter regulation within Europe on money laundering and corruption.

Mr. Mader presented the new Swiss Law on Return of Illicit Assets, making it easier for assets to be repatriated in the future. However, it also became clear that this was only the case if the states involved fell under the definition of 'failed states'. Should the victim country not initiate legal proceedings the newly introduced legislation in Switzerland would not be applicable. As a result, the Swiss law should only be seen as subsidiary measure that comes to play should international co-operation turn out unsuccessful.

Mr. Mader also presented measures that are important for the recovery of stolen assets, such as monitoring the use of such assets. As such, civil society and NGOs outside the jurisdiction of the victim country can facilitate the asset recovery processes, arbitrate with donors and do advocacy work at the international level. This is turn would result in the shift of balance in political interests; enable the negotiation of independent monitoring of returned assets, and the development of policy recommendations.

1. The importance of furthering research into what CSOs have done and should be doing, including monitoring of returned assets.
2. The need for training of CSOs in topics that are dealt within the asset recovery processes.
3. Increase advocacy efforts on changes in the legal frameworks in combating corruption and in asset recovery. This would include work on questions such as sharing damages and returned funds with the victim countries, creation of model legislation and disclosure requirements.
4. The investigative side of the work of CSOs was also re-emphasised, as the powers that CSOs have in publishing information cannot be underestimated.
5. In an effort to take this investigative role one step further, the panel also advocated for stronger efforts to promote CSOs becoming involved in litigation as third parties. The importance of working closely together with a network of lawyers and to further expand such a network was also discussed.

Academia

The academia panel consisted of Melvin Ayogu from *Standard Bank Global Leadership Centre*, Denise Umuhoza, *University of Tecnology Sydney* (Australia), Guillermo Jorge from the *University of San Andreas* (Argentina), and Michael Levi from the *University of Cardiff* (United Kingdom). Pedro Gomes Pereira, from the Basel Institute on Governance, moderated the session.

The panel dealt with the contributions academia can make to the asset recovery process. One important point that was raised was the research contributions that academia provides to other non-state and state actors, especially because some advocacy campaigns and investigations had been triggered by academic research in the past. Members of the academia panel also made it clear that corruption and asset recovery are not stand-alone topics but have to be put into context. Amongst the connected issues are organised crime and money laundering. It also became clear that a purely analytical approach might not always yield the desired or appropriate results.

Academia must not, for this reason, loose touch with the central question of how to actually change things. As a result, the panel concluded that there is a strong need for studies on impacts of the interventions within the asset recovery process, e.g., understanding what monies arising from settlement from corruption cases are used for by governments. The panellists agreed that a basic study resulting in a list of countries where civil society can actually bring cases and would have a standing before court would be beneficial.

More specifically, Mr. Ayogu and Ms. Umuhoza emphasised on the need of supporting research that would in turn encourage appropriate action in the asset recovery process. Areas that could be of interest include financial transparency, mutual legal assistance and extraterritorial application of the law, co-operation between public and private sectors, and increased financial and technical assistance to developing countries.

Mr. Jorge touched upon the issue that corruption is not the same everywhere, and as such there is a need to understand where the money is coming from and where it is going to in the corruption cycle.

Such knowledge would allow tackling the problem and guide action and reform within countries.

Finally, Prof. Levi alerted to the fact that in the world of criminology people seem to be obsessed with metrics – research demonstrated through statistical evidence. However, science hardly helps the efforts against corruption or the advocacy role. Thus, Prof. Levi advocated that data must be used in a pragmatic way, e.g., number of cases, amount of recovered assets every year and realistic figures of asset recovery. This way, it would be able to assess the harm that corruption and organised crime is doing to a country.

1. List and study of countries where civil society could bring cases/would have standing
2. More reliable studies on impacts of asset recovery
3. What is the cost of organised crime vs. asset recovery figures: what is the criminal asset gap?

Private sector

The private sector panel consisted of Otmar Hasler, former Prime Minister of Lichtenstein, KRP Group, Juanita Olaya, Director of the Basel Institute on Governance (Switzerland) and Markus E. Schulz from Zurich Insurance (Switzerland). Juanita Olaya also moderated the session.

Discussions centred on questions of responsibilities of the private sector and due diligence. Mr Hasler emphasised that Lichtenstein already at an early stage showed is commitment to anti-money laundering. Moreover, he explained that there was also a need to focus on education of private sector clients. He pointed out there are currently two problems: (i) tax evasion, and (ii) assets stolen by PEPs.

Mr. Schulz pointed out that the corruption agenda became important only just recently on the agenda of insurance companies. One of the challenges that this insurance sector faces is the need for self-regulation, as they are concerned about smaller, day-to-day transactions. The challenge for Mr. Schulz, however, it the loss in competitive power, as not all insurance companies are worried about corruption. Finally, Mr. Schulz emphasised a need to define PEPs, as it is not know who they should be, and during which period.

All of the panellists agreed that in a complex and rapidly changing world, all the drivers of the asset recovery process are interlinked and therefore, the private industry has to come on board in co-ordination. During the discussions, the panellists expressed a need to co-operate with other NSAs, especially in order to obtain information on new trends in corruption and asset recovery, and to exchange data and knowledge. Informal networks were mentioned as one possible option to drive the agenda further.

1. Need for collaboration and dialogue with other NSAs
2. Harmonisation between data protection regulations and anti-money laundering obligations

Service providers

The service providers panel consisted of Edward Davis Jr, Astigarraga Davis (United States), Chrisol Correia, Dow Jones Factiva (United Kingdom) and Klaus Fischer, Deloitte & Touche GmbH (Germany) and Dimitri Vlassis, UNDOC.

Right from the start, Mr. Vlassis made the point that asset recovery is an obligation much more than something that should be investigated according to a cost/benefit analysis. As a result, assisting in the recovery of stolen assets is much more a duty than something that can be chosen to do out of good will and when there is time and resources available. Mr. Vlassis pointed out that partnership opportunities between the public and private sectors – multi-stakeholder initiatives must be sought. Members of the panel welcomed the fact that civil routes of recovering assets were becoming more popular. It was however pointed out that corruption remained a crime and should therefore be prosecuted criminally.

Mr. Davis pointed out the importance of having the victim country wants to get out of the case, defining the 'win' from the beginning. Furthermore, there is a need to make use of civil asset recovery teams, comprised of lawyers, forensic accountants and investigators. Furthermore, asset recovery should focus on the values and not solely on the assets.

Mr. Correia informed how data providers assist in identifying PEPs. The challenge, however, is the fact that there is no definition of PEPs, while there is a need for regular screening, increasing the regulatory requirements and thus the operational impact of filtering PEP lists. Another challenge is the fact that there are difficulties associated with the transliteration of names between different alphabets, making it more difficult to locate PEPs.

Mr. Fischer pointed out that practitioners in the asset recovery field should understand the different legal avenues available to recover assets, and structure an investigation team accordingly. Mr. Fischer emphasised the need to have a good mix of legal and investigative skills in the investigation team.

Regarding PEPs, different NSAs during the meeting expressed that PEP screening is an extremely useful contribution to recovering assets, while others tended towards the fact the PEP screening was resource intensive and did not produce meaningful results. In the end, the panel agreed that follow-on cooperation between the different actors was crucial and that further ideas on data creation should be discussed.

1. Need for clearer definition of PEPs that can be used reliably by the service providers.
2. Need to establish clear goals when initiating the asset recovery processes to obtain maximum results.

Media

The media panel consisted of Michael Peel, Financial Times (United Kingdom), Omoyele Sowore, Sahara Reporters (United States), Laeticia Luvuezo, Canal Tin Television (DRC) and Alan Bacarese, Basel Institute on Governance (Switzerland).

In this panel, it very quickly became clear how the different groups can actually benefit from each other. Journalists made it clear that often, their stories are based on initial information they received from CSOs or individuals. Journalists are also interested in the expert knowledge lawyers possess, in order to be able to explain corruption investigations from a legal point of view. Nevertheless, it was shown that the media's role in asset recovery has to take into account the wider public interests: Media will only report about cases of corruption and asset recovery if people are interested in hearing about them. As a result, an element of entertainment cannot be ignored, even in the most serious cases.

Mr. Peel informed that a good story comprises of (i) large sums; (ii) interesting spending habits; (iii) tells us something bigger about how the world and corruption works; and (iv) have an international political dimension. However, Mr. Peel questioned what is the role of the journalist beyond this should be.

Mr. Sowore spoke about the *Sahara Reporters*, which takes the approach of the citizen reporter. The *Sahara reporter* focuses on property of Nigerian public officials, publishing public records, parties and Nigerian students which attend expensive schools abroad, among others. *Sahara Reporters* has the collaboration of the population in general, civil society and other media sources to public raw information. It has combined the power of the people and the internet – and has been able to transform the access to information in Nigeria.

Ms. Luvuezo informed that investigating corruption in the DRC has many challenges, as it costs too much, there is lack of access to information, lack of capacity and no partnership with other media sources throughout the world. Most of the investigated cases suffer from lack of freedom of information. She thus informed that the way forward would be to establish co-operation mechanisms to help manage restrictions on access to information. In such a way, the media can help investigators in publishing information they don't have a lead for; and (ii) in assisting tracing assets, as the media could publish publicly available information in order to obtain further collaboration for the investigation.

The media panel came up with several suggestions for ways forward. They discussed building networks between the victim and recipient countries. Such a co-operation between the media in each of these countries would enable a closer and more efficient monitoring process. Also ties between journalists would allow for an informal exchange of information, which might be especially valuable for countries in which there is only limited freedom of the press and certain things cannot be published. It was also examined how Anti- corruption Lawyers and journalist could work together more closely. The panelists were convinced that this cooperation would be valuable for both sides. Therefore, they advocated for an institutionalization of such kind of networks to make exchange more efficient and targeted.

1. Setting up informal networks to further exchange information to help the flow of information amongst journalists
2. Increase the collaboration between the media and NSAs to ensure accountability.

VALENTIN ZELLWEGER

Introduction*

Corrupt practices have long been accepted as a fact of life and inalienable part of any governmental power structure. Public funds are stolen and embezzled in all parts of the world and all countries, big or small, rich or poor. Nonetheless, in the past two decades, the international community has deployed considerable means in bringing an end to the phenomenon. And progress has been made. Just consider, a few years back, formal tax deductions for bribes paid by domestic companies in other countries were common practice in export-oriented economies. Not only have such incentives been repealed in the meantime but those countries have also criminalised the payment of bribes in other jurisdictions. The adoption of the United Nations Convention Against Corruption (UNCAC) by the UN General Assembly on 31 October 2003 has brought the fight against corruption to a universal level and has greatly enhanced the prospects of eradicating corrupt practices.

UNCAC provides for a general obligation of States Parties to prevent and combat corruption. States have to legislate accordingly. They also have a duty to co-operate with a view to returning stolen assets to the countries of origin. A whole chapter of UNCAC is devoted to that topic (chapter V, comprising 9 articles). According to these provisions, proceeds of corruption confiscated by one state shall be, if possible, returned to their prior legitimate owners, in most cases their state of origin.

Over the past years, numerous states have complemented their internal legislation, not least by implementing the recommendations of the Financial Action Task Force (FATF) pertaining to the fight against corruption, at home and abroad. National authorities have taken an array of measures which can roughly be divided in five categories: First and foremost a general commitment to prevent corruption. Sec-

* The views expressed herein are those of the author alone and do not necessarily reflect the position of the Federal Department of Foreign Affairs of Switzerland.

ond, different legal instruments were enacted to ensure that assets of illicit origin are prohibited from penetrating financial centres ('due diligence requirements'). The third element is an obligation to report suspicious transactions: Banks and financial intermediaries must inform the authorities as soon as they become aware of dubious dealings. If there is reason to believe that there may be a case of corruption, the criminal authorities must be alerted; they may then decide to initiate proceedings for money laundering. Mutual legal assistance in criminal matters is another powerful tool: at the request of the country in which the suspicious assets originate, funds can be frozen and if necessary returned to the country of origin on the basis of a formal application for mutual assistance. Finally the fifth pillar for combating illegal assets is their recovery and restitution to their rightful owners.

However, experience has shown that even with the most complete legislation, additional efforts are necessary to build successful asset recovery cases. For if they are to have any real impact, even the best legislative measures must first be brought to life. In addition, there must be a clear and unmistakeable political will of the government and the authorities involved to ensure the successful recovery of stolen assets. A proactive approach is required to overcome the hurdles of complex recovery cases; it is an illusion to think that the mere ratification of UNCAC will lead to lower corruption rates and larger sums of restitution.

To the public, asset recovery cases tend to look like pure government-to-government affairs. But other actors may have a role to play, either to support and assist governments or to supplement them. In fact, successful cases build on a convergence of different factors that involve other players, be they governmental (apart from national authorities, intergovernmental organisations such as the World Bank, the United National Development Programme (UNDP), the United Nations Office on Drugs and Crime (UNODC) as well as the joint World Bank/UNODC sponsored Stolen Asset Recovery Initiative), be they non-state actors.

In fact, mainly the latter play an often overlooked role in the fight against corrupt practices and the recovery of assets: By raising awareness of the destructive effects of corruption, the media put authorities under pressure to act; thus, many prominent cases have been triggered by courageous journalists and media outlets. Banks and financial intermediaries increasingly recognise the reputational risks involved in dealing with stolen funds. They have a central role to play in curbing corruption by applying due diligence standards and by reporting suspicious transactions to the prosecutorial authorities. Researchers and academics have documented the extent of corruption and its dramatic effects on the development of societies and the rule of law. Lawyers assist governments seeking the recovery of stolen assets in foreign jurisdictions or in cases that are easier to solve through litigation than sometimes cumbersome and lengthy mutual legal assistance proceedings. Non-governmental organisations have publicly denounced corruption, rallied political support and advocated stronger action by governments. Apart from their fight against endemic corruption, NGOs have also helped build political.

It is high time to emphasise the role of non-state actors in the recovery of stolen assets, to analyse their manifold contributions and to start a discussion about the potential for enhancing the co-operation between themselves as well as their interaction with governments. 'Non-State Actors in Asset Recovery', published by the Basel Institute on Governance, comprises for the first time contributions by experts representing different players involved in asset recovery. It thus fills an important lacuna in the growing corpus of publications about the recovery of stolen funds. It can only be hoped that this publication will trigger a discussion that will lead to a deeper understanding of the complex process of successful asset recovery.

Increased knowledge about the factors that decide over success or failure is essential as we are only at the beginning of a huge endeavour: According to StAR estimates, illicit funds associated with bribes received by public officials from developing and transition countries alone are estimated at USD 20 billion to USD 40 billion per year – a figure equivalent to 20 to 40 percent of flows of official development assistance. In the past decades, an estimated total of USD 4.5 billion has been restored to the countries of origin, USD 2 billion by Switzerland alone. In other words, despite all efforts, only an infinite fraction of all stolen funds has so far been recovered and restored to its rightful owners.

To know who can do what to increase that figure is crucial.

Amb. Valentin Zellweger
Director
Directorate of International Law, Federal Department of Foreign Affairs

Contributors

KODJO ATTISSO is Togolese and has been living in Switzerland since 2005. He holds a Bachelor's degree in civil law and a Master's degree in business law from the Université du Bénin (now known as Université de Lomé). He also holds a Master of Advanced Studies in Economic Crime Investigation from the Institut de Lutte contre la Criminalité Economique, in Neuchâtel, Switzerland. Since 2009, Kodjo is a Researcher/Project Support Officer at the International Centre for Asset Recovery (ICAR) of the Basel Institute on Governance.

MELVIN AYOGU is a Fellow, Africa Growth Initiative at Brookings Institution, Washington DC. His work focuses on economic development and value recovery of stolen assets. Melvin was Director, Global Leadership Centre at Standard Bank Group South Africa. Previously he served variously as Dean Faculty of Commerce University of Cape Town, Director of the School of Economics and professor of economics at the University of Cape Town. He was also the Convenor of the AERC-Collaborative PhD program in Economics at the University of Cape Town, a Rhodes Visiting African Scholar to Oxford University in 1995, and concurrently Visiting Scholar at the Centre for International Development and Senior Rockefeller Humanities Institute Fellow at Harvard University in 2000. Dr. Ayogu is an Associate of the Chartered Institute of Financial Services, London and serves on the Economic Advisory Board of the Task Force on Global Financial Integrity.

EDWARD DAVIS, JR. is a founding shareholder of the international law firm Astigarraga Davis in Miami, and heads its Asset Recovery and Financial Fraud Group which represents victims of serious fraud and grand corruption through investigating and prosecuting civil fraud matters around the world. He is a Certified Fraud Examiner and a member of the International Association of Financial Crime Investigators. He is Past Chair of the Florida Bar International Law Section, a member of the Anti-Corruption, International Litigation and Inter-American Law Committees of the International Law Section of the

American Bar Association; Vice Chair of the Anti-Corruption Committee of the International Bar Association; and he is a leading member of the London-based ICC Commercial Crimes Services FraudNet Network. Ed is currently lead counsel representing the Government of Trinidad and Tobago in a foreign public corruption case pending in Miami, Florida and has carriage of supervising other offshore proceeds of crime litigation in that case. He also acted as lead counsel for the Government of Antigua & Barbuda in proceeds of corruption litigation in the United States and elsewhere. Lastly, Ed is lead asset recovery counsel for the Custodian of BanCafe International Barbados, including having filed on behalf of the Custodian the first Chapter 15 bankruptcy petition in Florida, and Co-General Counsel to the Stanford International Bank Antigua Liquidation.

PEDRO GOMES PEREIRA is a lawyer and a member of the Brazilian Bar Association. He has previously worked in the Brazilian central authority for international co-operation, where he assisted authorities worldwide in co-ordinating their international strategies to combat organised crime, money laundering and corruption cases. Pedro joined the ICAR in June 2009 as an Asset Recovery Specialist.

MICHAEL LEVI is Professor of Criminology at Cardiff University. He has been conducting international research on the control of white-collar and organised crime, corruption and money laundering/ financing of terrorism since 1972, and has published widely on these subjects. He has recently completed a 3 year Professorial Fellowship from the UK's Economic and Social Science Research Council to examine the globalisation of economic crime and its control. He is Vice-President and President-elect of the US White-Collar Crime Research Consortium. Public roles in recent years include adviser to the UK Prime Minister's Strategy Unit and National Fraud Authority, the Home Office and Audit Commission; and adviser to the European Commission and Council of Europe. His most recent book is a revised monograph of his doctoral thesis, The Phantom Capitalists. He recently completed a study for the World Bank on Laundering of proceeds of corruption and its control within developing countries.

NICHOLAS LORD is a doctoral researcher in the School of Social Sciences at Cardiff University. His research interests include bribery and corruption, white-collar and corporate crime, financial crime and regulation theory. His PhD research examines the regulation of corporate bribery in international business transactions in the UK and Germany with analytical focus on the negotiation of regulation through an admixture of enforcement and non-enforcement mechanisms.

ANNE LUGON-MOULIN has a licence in Economics from the University of Fribourg and a Master of Arts in Economic Development and Policy Analysis from the University of Nottingham. Anne Lugon-Moulin has started her career with the Swiss State Secretariat for Economic Affairs. She then joined Transparency International to establish the Swiss Chapter in 1999. After that, she gained humanitarian field experience by working with the UN World Food Programme in Rwanda until 2003, when she then started to work for the Swiss Agency for Development and Cooperation (SDC) as Deputy Head of the Governance Section, responsible, among other tasks, for the anti-corruption agenda of SDC and the governance mainstreaming strategy. In 2008, she obtained an unpaid leave from SDC in order to hold the position of co-executive director of the Basel Institute on Governance. Anne further deepened her knowledge and experience in anti-corruption, governance and asset recovery. In 2010, she moved back to SDC where she took the position of Deputy Head of CIS countries Division. Among other tasks, she's responsible for addressing corruption and governance issues in the Division's entire portfolio. She has been recently appointed as co-head of the CIS Division as of end of 2011.

MAX MADER held degrees in Philosophy, Ethnology and Not-for-Profit Management. He was Managing Co-Director of Aktion Finanzplatz Switzerland where he coordinated international NGO campaigns for asset recovery and for transparent use of returned assets. In the Abacha and Mobutu cases, he worked on the premises as facilitator and supplier of information. He was member of the Duvalier coalition. He was delegate expert of the Swiss NGO coalition at the hearings for the Swiss draft act on stolen assets and coordinated the work group on international NGO recommendations for sustainable asset recovery.

KEITH OLIVER is a Senior Partner at Peters & Peters and heads the firm's specialist Commercial Litigation/Civil Fraud and Asset Tracing Team. He specialises in international and domestic civil and commercial fraud litigation, asset tracing/ recovery, regulatory, insolvency and trust litigation. Keith is recognised as one of the leading experts in civil fraud and asset tracing with extensive experience at the cutting edge of domestic and international fraud and asset tracing litigation (including the use of emergency procedures (freezing orders, search and seizure orders, passport orders). He is frequently engaged in multi-jurisdictional actions in the USA, continental Europe and worldwide.

MAUD PERDRIEL-VAISSIÈRE holds a Master of Laws (DEA) in International Law from the University of Assas, Paris. She is the managing director of SHERPA, a Paris-based group of anti-corruption advocates, which she joined in 2007 as a legal advisor within the 'Illicit capital flows' programme. Before joining SHERPA, Maud Perdriel-Vaissière volunteered at Global Witness within the 'Ending impunity Campaign'. Her main areas of expertise are sovereign debt, corporate tax evasion, grand corruption in resource-rich countries; and related public interest litigations. Maud also authored articles in books, academic journals and newspapers.

ANJA ROTH is a graduate of the Irish Centre for Human Rights in Galway and joined the Basel Institute on Governance as a Researcher/ Project Support Officer in September 2009. She holds an LLM in International Human Rights Law and a BA in European Studies from the University of Maastricht in the Netherlands. Anja worked with different international organisations like Amnesty International New Zealand and the Organization for Democratic Institutions and Human Rights (OSCE/ODIHR) in Warsaw.

MARKUS E. SCHULZ is the Group Head Financial Crime and the Chief Compliance Officer Global Life at Zurich Insurance. Markus joined Zurich in January 2008 after 13 years at ABN AMRO Bank, where he held various senior global Compliance positions, including Global Head Compliance Service Center and COO AML Compliance, as Corporate Senior Vice President and a member of the Global Compliance Management Team. Prior to his time in Compliance he served in a variety of senior in-country, Regional and Global management positions in the Back-, Mid- and Front-Office located in Germany, UK and the Netherlands for almost a decade. He was an active member of multiple Banking industry Compliance groups, like the Wolfsberg Group, and is providing his thought leadership to various Insurance and Compliance fora and other Think Tanks. Today he works with the Basel

Institute on Governance, CEA, FATF, International Anti-Corruption Academy and the Egmont group amongst others. Markus also is a very frequent and regular presenter, panelist, key note speaker, moderator and chairman at Compliance, AML, Anti-Financial Crime and Anti-Fraud conferences in Europe, Middle-East and the US. Markus is also an Advisory Board member of ACAMS®, the well known Association of Certified Anti-Money Laundering Specialists®.

DANIEL THELESKLAF is a lawyer by profession. After a career in the private sector at Swiss Life and Dresdner Bank, he joined the Swiss Federal Office of Police in 1998 to become the first Director of Switzerland's FIU. In 2002/2003, he led the Due Diligence Unite (the AML regulator) in Liechtenstein and, since 2000, he has been a board member of Transparency International, Switzerland. He is now engaged in various anti-money laundering, counter-terrorist financing and anti-corruption projects ant technical assistance missions for the OECD, the UN, the Council of Europe, the OSCE and the IMF.

ABOUT THE BASEL INSTITUTE ON GOVERNANCE

The Institute and its International Centre for Asset Recovery

The Basel Institute on Governance is an independent non-profit think tank conducting research, policy development and capacity building in the areas of corporate and public governance, anti-corruption and asset tracing and recovery. Based in Basel, Switzerland, and associated with the University of Basel, the Institute co-operates with governments and non-governmental organisations from around the world. Notably, the Institute also acts as a facilitator in debates on delicate corporate governance issues. In this context it co-founded the World Economic Forum's Partnering against Corruption Initiative and was central to the creation of anti-money laundering standards of the Wolfsberg Group.

The Institute's International Centre for Asset Recovery (ICAR) founded in July 2006 assists authorities in enhancing their capacities to seize, confiscate and recover the proceeds of corruption and money laundering. For this purpose, the ICAR trains officials in theoretical and strategic case assistance and facilitates co-operation between law enforcement agencies of different jurisdictions. In support of these activities, the ICAR operates a web-based knowledge sharing and training tool, the Asset Recovery Knowledge Centre (www.assetrecovery.org).

Basel Institute on Governance
International Centre for Asset Recovery
Steinenring 60, 4051 Basel, Switzerland
Phone +41 61 205 55 11, Fax +41 61 205 55 19
www.baselgovernance.org, info@baselgovernance.org

DANIEL THELESKLAF AND PEDRO GOMES PEREIRA

Acknowledgements

We would like to extend our warm appreciation to the authors for their expert contributions to this publication. It would not have been possible to have accomplished such a publication without their inputs.

Our gratitude is also extended to the Swiss Agency for Development and Co-operation (SDC). The Institute has only been able to undertake this project through the generous funding provided both for the experts' meeting hosted at the headquarters of the International Anti Corruption Academy (IACA) in Laxenburg, Austria, in September 2010 and for the publication of this book. The meeting in Laxenburg had not been possible with the overwhelming support we received from IACA) in particular from Martin Kreutner and his team.

Finally, our warm thanks go to Nina Schild, Anja Roth and Kodjo Attisso from the Institute. They have played a crucial role in the editing, layout and type setting of this publication.

ICAR would not be able to operate without critical seed funding from the SDC, UK Department for International Development (DfID) and the Government of Liechtenstein. We remain grateful to our funders for their financial support which enables us to undertake projects such as this publication, among many other projects of equal significance to the asset recovery agenda.

Daniel Thelesklaf
Director, International Centre for Asset Recovery

Pedro Gomes Pereira
Asset Recovery Specialist, International Centre for Asset Recovery

Abbreviations

ACT	Artemisinin-Based Combination Therapies
ADPHE	Asociación pro Derechos Humanos de España
AIDS	Acquired Immunodeficiency Syndrome
AML	Anti-Money Laundering
AREN	Asset Recovery Expert's Network
BMA	Bien Mal Acquis
CAAT	Campaign Against Arms Trade
CHF	Swiss Franc
CICA	UK Crime (International Co-operation) Act 2003
COCI	Composite Organised Crime Index
CoE	Council of Europe
CoSP	Conference of States Parties to the United Nations Convention Against Corruption
CPI	TI Corruption Perception Index
CSD	Centre for the Study of Democracy
CSO	Civil-Society Organisations
DfID	UK Department for International Development
DRC	Democratic Republic of the Congo
DTO	Drug Trafficking Organisation
EC	European Commission
EU	European Union
EUR	Euro (currency)
FATF	Financial Action Task Force
FCPA	US Foreign Corrupt Practices Act 1977
FDFA	Swiss Federal Department of Foreign Affairs
FDI	Foreign Direct Investment
FDJ	Swiss Federal Department of Justice
FIU	Financial Intelligence Unit

FOJ	Swiss Federal Office of Justice
FOM	Swiss Federal Office for Migration
G20	The Group of Twenty Finance Ministers and Central Bank Governors
GBP	British Pound Sterling
GFI	Global Financial Integrity
IACA	International Anti-Corruption Academy
ICAR	International Centre for Asset Recovery
ICC	International Chamber of Commerce
IFI	International Financial Institutions
IGO	International Governmental Organisations
MDG	Millennium Development Goals
MLA	Mutual Legal Assistance
NGO	Non-Governmental Organisation
NORAD	Norwegian Agency for Development and Co-operation
NSA	Non-State Actor
OCTA	EU Organised Crime Threat Assessment
ODA	Official Development Assistance
OECD Anti-Bribery Convention	OECD Convention on Combating Bribery of Foreign Public Officials in International Business Transactions
OSJI	Open Society Justice Initiative
PACE 1984	UK Police and Criminal Evidence Act
PACI	Partnering Against Corruption Initiative
PIL	Public Interest Litigation
POCA	UK Proceeds of Crime Act 2002
RIAA	Swiss Federal Act on the Restitution of Assets of Politically Exposed Persons obtained by Unlawful Means
SFO	UK Serious Fraud Office
SOCA	UK Serious Organised Crime Agency
StAR	Stolen Asset Recovery Initiative
TI	Transparency International
UDEMO	Union Démocratique des Mobutistes
UK	United Kingdom
UN	United Nations

UNCAC	United Nations Convention Against Corruption
UNCITRAL	United Nations Commission on International Trade Law
UNDP	United Nations Development Programme
UNODC	United Nations Office on Drugs and Crime
US	United States of America
USD	US Dollar
WB	World Bank
WEF	World Economic Forum
WLAN	Wireless Local Area Network
Wolfsberg Principles	Wolfsberg Anti-Money Laundering Principles on Private Banking

Pedro Gomes Pereira, Anja Roth and Kodjo Attisso

A stronger role for non-state actors in the asset recovery process

I. What are non-state actors (NSAs)?

When talking about NSAs, one very quickly comes to realise that this concept caters for a wide range of potential candidates that might qualify for its label. As a result, it makes sense to define what is meant by the term before starting to talk about the different roles of NSAs. It has become clear recently, that the classical nation state alone can no longer be seen as the sole bearer of power and sovereignty in a country. It is no longer the only source of regulation and norm formation. The influence of NSAs has been accepted widely today and it has been recognised that 'there has been an increasing insertion of non-state actors […] in global governance.' [1,2]

Looking for a comprehensive description of the term NSAs, one cannot get around the definition that is given in the Cotonou Agreement, and that has been accepted widely and is used internationally today. In its Article 6, dealing with 'definitions', NSAs include, 'the private sector, economic and social partners including trade union organisations and civil society in all its forms according to national characteristics.' The same article also mentions some limitations and how potential NSAs can be filtered, namely according to 'the extent to which they address the needs of the population, […] their specific

1 A. Reinisch, 'The Changing International Legal Framework for Dealing with Non State Actors', in Palston, *Non State Actors and Human Rights*, Oxford University Press, 2005, p. 74.

2 I. Ul Haque, *Non-State Actors and Global Governance*, p. 2.

competencies, [and] whether they are organized and managed democratically and transparently.'[3]

On its side, The European Commission through its Communication on the Participation of Non-State Actors in EU Development Policy defines NSAs as 'a range of organisations that bring together the principal, existing or emerging, structures of the society outside the government and public administration.'[4] As for the European Financing Instrument of Cooperation and Development, a precise and detailed list of NSAs is provided in its article 24.2. This includes 'non-governmental organisations, organisations representing indigenous peoples, organisations representing national and/or ethnic minorities, local traders' associations and citizens' groups, co-operatives, trade unions, organisations representing economic and social interests, organisations fighting corruption and fraud and promoting good governance, civil rights organisations and organisations combating discrimination, local organisations (including networks) involved in decentralised regional co-operation and integration, consumer organisations, women's and youth organisations, teaching, cultural, research and scientific organisations, universities, churches and religious associations and communities, the media and any non-governmental associations and independent foundations, including independent political foundations.'

The paragraph above already provides us with a first impression of what NSAs are, or could be. Further definitions can be drawn from the book Non-Sate Actors as Standard Setters, which describes NSAs as 'a broad term encompassing intergovernmental organisations, non-governmental organisations, transnational corporations, as well as new forms of mixed standard setters such as 'public private partnerships' (PPPs) or 'multi-shareholder groups''.[5] Büthe goes so far as to call

3 Second Revision of the Cotonou Agreement, Brussels, 11 March 2010. The Cotonou Agreement is the most comprehensive partnership agreement between developing countries and the EU. Since 2000, it has been the framework for the EU's relations with 79 countries from Africa, the Caribbean and the Pacific (ACP).

4 European Commission, *Communication on the Participation of Non-State Actors in EU Development Policy*, May 2003, p.5.

5 A. Peters, L. Koechlin, T. Förster & G. F. Zinkernagel *Non-State Actors as Standard Setters*, Cambridge University Press, New York, 2009, p. xix.

NSAs 'a residual category, comprising any actor that is not a state, including international governmental organisations (IGOs), NGOs, multinational corporations, formal and informal transnational networks of government bureaucrats, general public (opinion), international professional associations and commercial lobbying groups, as well as international criminal and terrorist networks.'[6] This is a rather wide definition and for the purposes of this book, NSAs will later be narrowed down to five very specific groups of actors.

The abovementioned EU development policy obviously comes with many opportunities and an increase in diversity, which is usually desirable in democratic systems; however, it also bears certain challenges and pitfalls when questions of legitimacy and accountability are raised. Other than classical state actors that usually work within a system that is – at least formally – based on integrity, NSAs are a global phenomenon that has so far proven to be much harder to regulate. However, on the other side, NSAs themselves have contributed to increasing transparency by putting pressure on International Financial Institutions like the IMF and World Bank.[7] When talking about possible pitfalls, another point that should be kept in mind is the fact that today most NSAs come from developed and industrialised nations. As a result, one could argue that, 'the inclusion of NSAs [...] in global governance tips the scales further in favour of the industrial countries.'[8]

Hilary Clinton recently paid tribute to the growing importance of NSAs in the international arena; she emphasised the positive side-effects the emergence of this new set of actors can have in a globalised world and the importance those actors can carry when it comes to furthering democracy and human rights. In her article, she outlines the relevance of leadership through civilian power.[9] She sketches out the importance in diplomacy to connect 'with audiences outside of government, such as the private sector and civil society.'[10] Along the lines

6 T. Büthe, Governance through Private Authority: Non-State Actors in Global Governance, *Journal of International Affairs*, 2004, 58.1, p. 281.

7 ibid, p. 11.

8 ibid, p. 14.

9 H.R. Clinton, *Leading through Civilian Power: Redefining American Diplomacy*, Foreign Affairs Magazine 2010, p.1.

10 ibid, p. 2.

of the argumentation of this book, NSAs are increasingly becoming more important and 'are more able to influence current events.'[11] Throughout her whole article, it becomes clear that in today's world, notice does not only have to be taken of traditional state actors, but also of the many NSAs that might be evenly important in forming public opinion and ultimately also contribute to policy making in a specific context.

When trying to explain the phenomenon of the growing importance of NSAs, one possible explanation is the fact that today's world through globalisation has become more complex and, as a result, governments usually cannot specialise in all the areas that would be necessary to holistically approach certain issues. Consequently, NSAs manage to fill these gaps with their capacity to specialise in one specific area and to complement government's approaches and angles. Furthermore, in the area of development aid, experience over the years has shown that the involvement of local NSAs is crucial for the success of sustainable intervention and change. Accordingly, NSAs have increased their influence on and participation in development aid worldwide.

Turning to defining the different groups of NSAs that are specifically relevant for this publication, it first has to be made clear that those actors have been chosen according to their importance and potential in the asset recovery processes. Starting off with a group that bears tremendous potential for the cause of recovering assets that have been stolen, academia will be looked at in more detail. After that, a classical group of well-established NSAs are CSOs. Their importance and influence has already been outlined by national and international organisations in the past.[12] The media is another important player on the international stage. Of course, this, as all other groups, is not a homogeneous group which can be categorised easily especially when it comes to its aims and purposes, but the way in which the media exercises influence as a NSA can be described and analysed unambiguously. Financial institutions are NSAs that are particularly relevant

11 ibid, p. 3.

12 e.g. European Commission, *Communication on the Participation of Non-State Actors in EU Development Policy*, May 2003.

to asset recovery. This can also be said about the private sector. As a result, all these groups have been included in our analysis of NSAs.

Civil society organisations

CSOs are at the core of NSAs. They have a crucial role to play when it comes to public opinion forming, political lobbying, oversight functions and representation of public interests. In the area of peace-building for example, CSOs have been called 'important [...] in preventing violent conflict, crisis management and peace-building.'[13] In the area of international financial institutions, 'NGOs have helped to broaden the development agenda to include the social and environmental impact of the IFIs' activities and pressed to make the IMF and the World Bank more open and sensitive to public opinion.' Furthermore, 'the NGO community has raised important and pertinent questions on the orientation, strategies and programs for economic development. They helped to rise consciousness of issues and problems that governments and international development agencies might have otherwise finessed or neglected.'[14]

Academia

Academia has always been an important impetus for political and social change. Many important ideas that have later found their way into policy decisions and strategic political planning originated from academic research and output. The rich plurality of academic views on various subjects (governance, politics, economies, social, development, environment, etc.) contributes to understanding questions on specific areas. The role of the universities as NSAs in public policy is increasing. They facilitate and contribute decisively to the sustainability

13 International Alert – Saferworld Submission on the European Commission's Communication on the Participation of Non-State Actors in EU Development Policy, 2003, p. 2.

14 I. Ul Haque, *Non-State Actors and Global Governance*, p. 1, 11.

of policies processes, filling a key complementary role for activities conducted by other actors, both state and NSAs. Academia (universities, academic institutes, researches centres, scholars, etc.) is a group with skilled technical and human resources, and serves as a huge space of awareness and interest in spreading knowledge and values.

As proof of this increasing position and roles in strategies or policy shaping, more recently, the EU joined with the process of growing recognition of universities as actors in development co-operation and expressly includes universities as NSAs for development.[15] However, the role of academia may in certain situation be undermined or biased by the lure of attractive consultancies, usually commissioned by governments and donor agencies. These activities, lucrative as they are for the consultants, leave little time for serious teaching and also lead to intellectual compromise, as it becomes difficult to bite the hand that feeds one.[16]

Media

The importance of the media in contributing to government accountability as well as to informing public opinion is probably undisputed. So are also certain reservations that come to mind when thinking about the power the media can develop and exercise. Generally speaking however, the positive impact the media has had in the area of governance in general, tremendously adding to transparency and accountability, overbalances the negative sides of its impact and involvement on the global stage. Without courageous investigative journalists, many corruption scandals for example would have never been uncovered.

In many countries, and specifically in the majority of developing countries, the media has seen its importance rise exponentially over the past two decades, in tandem with the liberalisation of political and economic regimes. As a consequence, this has weakened the state monopoly as far as sources and the content of information are con-

15 European Commission Communication of 25 January 2006 (COM (2006) 19 final).

16 J. Ulimwengu, *The Role of Non-State Actors*, p. 7. http://www.afrimap.org/english/images/documents/AGFVII-Paper5-TheRoleofNon-StateActors.pdf.

cerned. In a significant number of countries, this new media reality (importantly internet, social network service, online service or platform, online database, etc.) has been instrumental in sensitising public opinion against corruption, graft and sleaze, offering a platform to political and social views previously muzzled and helping to curb official impunity in issues of misappropriation of public funds, of corruption and of human rights abuses.[17]

Financial institutions

Banks and other financial institutions and service providers also have a role to play aside from the role the state is playing. Their influence becomes most obvious in financial matters. Banks have great powers when it comes to granting credits to private persons as well as corporations. Furthermore, the international financial crisis has shown very plastically how influential banks can be for the global economy. One other category that illustrates the relevance of financial institutions are activities such like the Wolfsberg Group. This Group, which was born out of 'two leading banks that could be convinced by the NGO Transparency International and the think-tank Basel Institute on Governance to form the nucleus of a group whose aim it was to develop customer-due-diligence standards in private banking', is a good example of a private banking sector initiative.[18] The Wolfsberg Group developed compliance standards for the financial services industry.

The legal community

This category encompasses a wide range of actors, mainly involved in commercial pursuits. The role of law firms for example, is probably rather new for the researcher looking into the different NSAs. However, the weight of the private sector should not be underestimated.

17 J. Ulimwengu, *The Role of Non-State Actors*, p. 6.

18 M. Pieth, 'Multistakeholder Initiatives to Combat Money Laundering and Bribery', *Basel Institute on Governance, Working Paper Series No 2*, 2006. p. 6.

Lawyers representing victims of corruption have come to exercise a very important role. They combine the legal expertise and the necessary legitimacy to raise awareness to state and non-state violations of specific rights of individuals or the population as a whole.

II. Asset recovery and non-state actors

Understanding asset recovery is essential in order to identify the roles that NSAs play in it. The classical asset recovery process encompasses procedures that vary from intelligence gathering, undertaking financial investigations, seizing and freezing assets for subsequent confiscation, and the return of such assets. In turn, these steps within the asset recovery process are complex and depend not only on the political will to undertake such cases, on the one hand, but also relies on the ability of law enforcement agencies to proactively co-ordinate and collaborate with each other, on the other.

Furthermore, the criminal activity which links to a large scale asset recovery process typically occurs across multiple jurisdictions, and for this reason there is a need for the affected jurisdictions to be able to project their jurisdictions externally in order to allow for the best strategy to be pursued. Here, a high degree of political will, resources and expertise is necessary to carry out such tasks.

These factors make the asset recovery process immensely intricate, time-consuming and resource intensive (ICAR, 2011). One of the difficulties is that of the traditional approach to repressing criminal activity through criminal law. It focuses on the commission of the criminal offence by its perpetrator, seeking his or her conviction. The traditional approach is insufficient when considering the return of proceeds of crime through asset recovery, as the unlawful gains which stem from the criminal offence is given little attention in the criminal proceedings, generally being seen as a complicated, difficult and an ancillary matter (StAR, 2009).

Criminalising money laundering began shifting the traditional approach of criminal law to also include the proceeds resulting from the criminal offence. With money laundering, the perpetrator attempts to disguise the true nature, origin and ownership of the proceeds derived from criminal activities (e.g., corruption), which in turn is predicate to the money laundering offence. These unlawful proceeds provide the common link between the criminal activity of money laundering and asset recovery, as both will occur once the predicate offence has taken place (ICAR, 2011).

No longer were the proceeds to be seen as an ancillary matter in the criminal proceedings and law enforcement needed to provide an appropriate response. The asset recovery process thus required a change in the mind-set of the approach taken by law enforcement to repress crime. Thus, an effective, integrated approach (StAR, 2009) must be envisaged on a case-by-case scenario, in which the options for action available must be factored in. The establishment of this comprehensive strategy, however, depends of specific areas that must communicate and intertwine to produce the desired results.

However, this comprehensive strategy approach also faces numerous obstacles. Precisely identifying the stolen funds and the total amount derived from the criminal offence often hamper asset recovery efforts. These require specialised knowledge, e.g., on financial investigations and forensic accounting, to prove the illicit nature of the assets. Other obstacles include overcoming the inconsistent legal requirements that exist across jurisdictions, the lack of technical capacities in the asset recovery process within and abroad, the lack of political will in the jurisdictions involved, and the lack of co-ordination between national and foreign agencies (ICAR, 2011).

The greatest limitation, however, is that oftentimes the authorities involved in the asset recovery processes do not have the necessary expertise or information which would otherwise allow for an efficient case. Here, the role of NSAs is quite noticeable. The active and proactive participation of the private sector, for example, assists states to gather the necessary intelligence which can then be cross-checked. It is for this reason that states themselves have recognised that, be it through the involvement of civil society (article 13 UNCAC), or the participation of the private sector and financial institutions in article 52 UNCAC, NSAs form the basis of a functioning society.

The report of the 3rd CoSP concluded that three basic conditions for the successful implementation of the UNCAC, and consequently of asset recovery, must be apparent: political will, sufficient resources and the active involvement of civil society.[19] Thus, the interaction of both state actors and NSAs is required in order to pursue the most effective policies to address the asset recovery agenda. This interaction, in turn, is to have a multi-faceted approach and response from both parties.

NSAs can perform several roles in the asset recovery process, either independently, concurrently or in co-ordination with states. This chapter will seek to name but a few of the possibilities of the work that is undertaken by the NSAs to bridge the gap or overcome some of the challenges in asset recovery. Thus, focus will be given to the following areas: (i) advocacy groups and mass media; (ii) management and monitoring; (iii) research and information gathering; (iv) capacity building; and (v) legal services.

Advocacy groups and mass media

Advocacy groups and mass media seek to ensure greater transparency and accountability for the actions conducted by states, NSAs and individuals, as well as to ensure the accountability of government to its citizens. Their work ensures the prevalence of the rule of law and enhances the freedom of information.

Mass media, in particular through the work of investigative journalism, allows for the uncovering of facts committed by a specific target group, which would otherwise not have come to light. The focus may be a potential criminal action conducted by a natural or a legal person, the unlawful gains derived by this person from the criminal action, or both.

19 Report of the Conference of the States Parties to the United Nations Convention against Corruption on its third session, held in Doha from 9 to 13 November 2009 (CAC/COSP/2009/15). Available at http://www.unodc.org/documents/treaties/UNCAC/COSP/session3/V0988538e.pdf.

Unlike an investigator, which must reveal the source of the information during the trial to ensure due process, journalists have the advantage that they have the possibility to ensure that their sources remain anonymous. This is of particular importance to the asset recovery processes, as sources (whether victims or whistle-blowers) may not have come forth with the information otherwise.

In turn, advocacy groups aim to influence the public policy by providing active support to a specific cause. Their motivation stems from moral or ethical principles aiming at protecting an interest. For this reason, they represent and give voice to interest of citizens and also mobilising them to participate in the democratic process. Advocacy groups play an essential role in the asset recovery processes, as they are able to indicate possible wrongdoing in inter-state interaction.

The activities undertaken by both the mass media and advocacy groups play an important role in the asset recovery processes, as it is through them that it may be possible to spark an investigation by state actors. These groups may help steer investigations in the right direction to ensure that briberies and its resulting proceeds are not overlooked.

Management and monitoring

NSAs also play a fundamental role in the areas of managing seized assets, as well as the oversight and monitoring of returned assets.

Within the asset recovery processes, once the proceeds and instrumentalities of crime have been identified, they must be seized so that they are not dissipated by the criminal perpetrators, thus losing all the effort of gathering intelligence and evidence of the whereabouts and origin of the assets.

However, the actual confiscation of assets can be time consuming, as these must be proven to be derived from criminal activity, and consequently a court order must be obtained. During this period in between the confiscation of the proceeds and instrumentalities of crime and their actual confiscation, the assets have to be managed (here understood as the management, including the sale of the property, any part of or interest in the property which has been seized) in order not to loose their value.

The maintenance of the value of the seized assets is of paramount importance, as the full amount is sought so it can be returned to its rightful owner (whether the victim or the bona fide third party). Courts and prosecutors do not always have the qualifications or the experience necessary to make important decisions relating to the management of the seized assets. Appointing someone with the experience and background in the area of management of seized assets – for example an accountant – becomes a viable solution. These professional managers remove the burden of management of seized assets from state actors.

Another challenge in which NSAs can assist state actors is in the actual return of the confiscated assets to the victim country. Previous experiences have shown that countries may impose conditions to minimise the possibility that these returned assets are once again stolen. NSA networks in both the victim country and the country that is returning the assets ensure that there is accountability in the use of these stolen assets, as well as transparency in the overall return of the assets.

Research and information gathering

Research conducted by academia, think tanks and service providers are fundamental as they can in turn trigger advocacy campaigns, media reports, and investigations. They also assist state actors and NSAs to better put the asset recovery process into context. In this sense, research can assist in identifying models of the processes in which a criminal activity occurs, and subsequently determine a model to combat it.

Combating corruption and money laundering, as well as the asset recovery processes have put in place a comprehensive set of regulations which require the retention of certain types of documentation, e.g., bank statements, for a certain period of time. This documentation is kept in order to prevent the commission of said offences, but also so that the paper trail may be used on financial investigations should a criminal offence be committed.

Notwithstanding, the use and manipulation of such sensitive information must be in line with rules and regulations pertaining to the protection of privacy and data. Here, research can assist such institutions and state actors to verify whether the regulation in place is in fact ensuring the protection of privacy. This research can also verify the consistency of the regulation as well as of the practices to provide for recommendations to make the entire system more effective.

This is because the asset recovery processes demand a high amount of data to be processed to minimise the incidence of the crime. Moreover, the perception of a transnational crime such as corruption is of great difficulty to combat at a global level, due to the fact that offence may not be perceived in another country, were the proceeds of crime ultimately end up, but which has no direct link with the place where the offence takes place.

NSAs have become critical in this area. They can assist state actors and other NSAs by providing indexes and other data comparing countries based on their risk to corruption and money laundering. Such is the case, for example, of the Corruption Perception Index prepared annually by TI.

NSAs can also assist state actors and other NSAs by collecting, processing and analysing publicly available information on persons. This turn will assist states, but particularly other NSAs in determining the level of risk of the client relationship with a person which may be a PEP in his or her country of origin.

Capacity building

One of the biggest challenges faced in the asset recovery processes is the lack of capacities faced by the authorities in the countries which must interact to obtain successful asset recovery. Thus, there is great need for building capacities locally so that it may be possible for the state and non-state actors alike to respond efficiently to the challenges of asset recovery.

NSAs bring forth their expertise in the various areas which comprise the asset recovery processes to build the necessary long-term capacities so that developing countries can adequately respond to the challenges and dynamism of the asset recovery processes. Furthermore, NSAs can assist to build the necessary institutions that can ensure efficient prevention and criminalisation of corruption through the asset recovery processes.

Moreover, NSAs not only assist developing countries in building their capacities, but also within the development community. This is because the asset recovery processes is a new concept in the development agenda. This thus requires raising awareness and understanding of the topic amongst donor practitioners. Through the awareness-raising, the donor community is better equipped to precise the needs of a country.

Legal services

This is another important form in which NSAs can assist in the asset recovery processes. Sometimes, the traditional approach to combating corruption is insufficient, and victim countries must take action through the use of private attorneys in the country in which the assets are to ensure that these seized, confiscated and ultimately repatriated.

Thus, there are two main aspects in which NSAs can assist in litigation. They can either represent a state actor in the courts of the state in which the assets or relevant evidence is (foreseen in article 53 UNCAC), or they may represent a group of persons which has an interest in ensuring that stolen assets from a specific target group in the victim state (which may have co-opted the government altogether) to seize stolen assets.

Legal practitioners and lawyers can provide important assistance to state actors in the establishment of their strategies to prevent and combat corruption, as well as to analyse the system as an external and independent eye towards seeking to find gaps in the asset recovery processes of a country or even recommendations in drafting legislation to adequately meet the international standards and local realities of the country. This is done especially when the local capacities for understanding of the asset recovery processes is insufficient.

NSAs are a fundamental force to enhance or create the necessary political will in the jurisdictions involved in an asset recovery case.

Past examples have shown that some countries do not have the necessary political will to ensure the effectiveness of asset recovery cases, e.g., the ruling political elite of a state has captured the state functions in order to ensure impunity for their criminal actions. Here, several approaches can be taken by the NSAs.

References

StAR. (2009). Stolen Asset Recovery: Towards a Global Architecture for Asset Recovery (pp. 1–73).

ICAR. (2011). Development Assistance, Asset Recovery and Money Laundering: MAKING THE CONNECTION (pp. 1–30).

A Reinisch, 'The Changing International Legal Framework for Dealing with Non State Actors', in Palston, Non State Actors and Human Rights, Oxford University Press, 2005.

I. Ul Haque, Non-State Actors and Global Governance.

A. Peters, L. Koechlin, T. Förster & G. F. Zinkernagel Non-State Actors as Standard Setters, Cambridge University Press, New York, 2009.

T. Büthe, Governance through Private Authority: Non-State Actors in Global Governance, Journal of International Affairs, 2004, 58.1.

H.R. Clinton, Leading through Civilian Power: Redefining American Diplomacy, Foreign Affairs Magazine 2010.

M Pieth, 'Multistakeholder Initiatives to Combat Money Laundering and Bribery', Basel Institute on Governance, Working Paper Series No 2, 2006.

J. Ulimwengu, The Role of Non-State Actors. available at http://www.afrimap.org/english/images/documents/AGFVII-Paper5-TheRoleofNon-StateActors.pdf.

MAUD PERDRIEL-VAISSIÈRE

How to turn Article 51 into reality?

'I will say that he has left nothing in anyone's house,
nothing even in the towns, nothing in public places,
not even in the temples, nothing in the possession of any Sicilian,
nothing in the possession of any Roman citizen;
that he has left nothing, in short,
which either came before his eyes or was suggested to his mind,
whether private property or public, or profane or sacred, in all Sicily.'
(Excerpts from 'Oratio de Signis', fourth speech against Verres[1]; Cicero – 70 BC).

Even more so than the average citizen, those holding public or elective office should be of unquestionable integrity.

It is not unheard of, however, for such individuals to profit unduly from their position so as to enrich themselves at the expense of the rest of society.

Corruption of public officials has been known since time immemorial, as illustrated by the famous Verres trial which made Cicero famous, and is probably a constant in all forms of political organisation. Indeed, 'it is unlikely that there has ever been a ruling class which did not exploit its political power to further its private financial interests.'[2]

Whenever ruling elites engage in wide-scale corruption and the systematic plundering of the state's resources, one might use the term

1 Verres was governor of Sicily (*propraetor*) from 73 to 70 B.C. A man of pleasure, corrupt and greedy, he treated the province as his personal possession. After he left office, Sicilians hired Cicero and sued him.

2 European Parliament 1995 Resolution on Combating Corruption in Europe, Explanatory Statement No. 2 (b); cited in Professor Ndiva Kofele-Kale, Good Governance as Political Conditionality, Democracy and Good Governance (ICASSRT, 1999).

'patrimonicide' or 'indigenous spoliation'.[3] Acts of indigenous spoliation include sale of government property by public officials, embezzlement of public funds, nepotism, bribery, extortion and tax exemptions that benefit the wealthy while harming the masses.

Such states or governments that practice large-scale corruption at the expense of the general populations are referred to as kleptocracies (from the Greek klepto, theft, and kratos, power); literally a government by thieves.[4]

Although in the past the accumulated wealth of corrupt leaders was mainly recycled locally, i.e., within the limits of the victim state, globalisation lead to increased internationalisation by allowing 'greater mobility of wealth and the capacity to hide and disguise it'.[5]

Long neglected due to focus on transnational corporate corruption,[6] this peculiar form of 'sovereign corruption' would come to be viewed as a matter of global concern in the light of the predatory regimes of Ferdinand Marcos (Philippines), general Suharto (Indonesia), or Mobutu Sese-Seko (DRC – formerly Zaire). The amounts of wealth stolen by these ruling families were so massive that an author described these depredations as going 'beyond shame and almost beyond imagination'.[7]

3 See Ndiva Kofele-Kale, *International Law of Responsibility For Economic Crimes: Holding Heads Of States And Other High Ranking State Officials Individually Liable For Acts Of Fraudulent Enrichment* (Kluwer Law International, 1995); See also Ndiva Kofele-Kale, *Patrimonicide: The International Economic Crime of Indigenous Spoliation*, 28 VAND. J. TRANS'L L. 45, 58 (January 1995).

4 Jennifer M. Hartman, *Government By Thieves: Revealing The Monsters Behind The Kleptocratic Masks*, 24 Syracuse J. Int'l L. & Com. 157 (1997).

5 Abram Chayes, *Pursuing the Assets of Former Dictators, in* Proceedings Of The 81st Annual Meeting Of The American Society Of International Law, p.395 (1987).

6 As expressed by Professor Michael Reisman in a 1989 piece that appeared in the American Journal of International Law, the *Ritual of condemnation of foreign corporations' spoliations of the resources of developing countries and their elevation to the level of international concern have obscured the problem of spoliations by national officials of the wealth of the states.* See W. Michael Reisman, *Harnessing International Law to Restrain and Recapture Indigenous Spoliations*, 83 AH. J. INT'L L. 56–57.

7 Darrel Delamaide, *The Debt Shock: The Full Story of the World Credit Crisis* p.60 (1984).

Developing countries hold no monopoly over corruption;[8] they do however suffer more acutely from it than developed countries.[9] According to a joint report from the WB and the UNODC, corrupt money associated with bribes received by public officials from developing and transition countries is estimated at USD 20 to USD 40 billion per year – a figure equivalent to 20 to 40 per cent of total ODA.[10]

That same report estimates that every USD 100 million returned to a developing country could fund equality: 3.3 to 10 million insecticide-treated bed nets, which are twice as effective as regular bed nets; first-line treatment for over 600,000 people for one year for HIV/AIDS; 50 to 100 million ACT treatments for malaria; full immunisation for 4 million children; approximately 250,000 water connections for households; or 240 kilometres of two-lane paved roads.[11]

With only four years left until the 2015 target date for achieving the eight MDGs,[12] the repatriation of stolen assets to victim countries

8 One only has to consider the numerous recent political and financial scandals in western countries: the trial of Jacques Chirac over embezzlement of public funds, the Parliamentary expenses in the UK, the Malaya operation in Spain…

9 The correlation between corruption and low development has been abundantly proven: P. Mauro, *Why Worry about corruption?*, Economic issues n° 6 : IMF (1997) ; P. Mauro, *The Effects of Corruption on Growth and Public Expenditure, in* Political Corruption: Concepts and Contexts, Eds. Heidenheimer A. & Johnson, M. (Transaction Publishers, 2002) ; Chetwynd, Eric, Frances Chetwynd, and Bertram Spector, *Corruption and Poverty: A Review of Recent Literature, Management Systems International*, (2003) ; J.G. Lambsdorff, *How corruption Affects Economic Development in* Global Corruption Report 2003: pp. 310–312; Boris Podobnik, Jia Shao, Djuro Njavro, Plamen Ch. Ivanov and H.E. Stanley, *Influence of corruption on economic growth rate and foreign investment*, Eur. Phys. J. B 63, 547–550 (2008).

10 Stolen Asset Recovery (StAR) Initiative: Challenges, Opportunities, and Action Plan, joint report from the World Bank and the United Nations Office on drugs and crime (UNODC), June 2007.

11 Op.cit p.11

12 The MDGs are eight international development goals that all 192 United Nations member states and at least 23 international organizations have agreed to achieve by the year 2015. They include eradicating extreme poverty, reducing child mortality rates, fighting disease epidemics such as AIDS, and developing a global partnership for development. More information at: http://www.un.org/millenniumgoals.

is becoming a major development issue, as underlined in 2002 in the Monterrey Consensus of the International Conference on Financing for Development.[13]

The international community seems to have assessed the importance of this issue since 2003 and has adopted the UNCAC (also known as the Merida Convention). The Convention dedicates a whole chapter to stolen asset recovery (Chapter V); Article 51 going as far as ranking it a 'fundamental principle'.[14]

Such a goal is in itself lofty. The difficulty, however, lies in the fact that this Convention, as all conventional instruments, is highly state-centrist: made by states, for states. In other words, and although the Merida Convention strongly reinforces the means of action available for asset recovery,[15] those means are only at the disposal of state entities.

What if the state's own public officials are involved in plundering the country's resources? What of Duvalier- (Haiti) or Mobutu-like (Zaire) situations, in which despite the removal of the corrupt agents, victim states are unable or unwilling to trigger and conduct the appropriate legal proceedings?

13 The Monterrey Consensus was the outcome of the 2002 Monterrey Conference, the United Nations International Conference on Financing for Development. Heads of State and Government adopted it on 22 March 2002. The full text of the consensus is available at: http://www.un.org/esa/ffd/monterrey/MonterreyConsensus.pdf. In 2008, a Follow-up International Conference on Financing for Development was held in Doha (Qatar) to Review the Implementation of the Monterrey Consensus. It reaffirmed the goals and commitments of the Monterrey Consensus. The full text of the Doha declaration is available at: http://daccess-dds-ny.un.org/doc/UNDOC/LTD/N08/630/55/PDF/N0863055.pdf?OpenElement.

14 Regarding the meaning and scope of this disposition, see *UNCAC legislative guide*: 'In spite of the fact that an interpretative note to the Convention indicating that the expression 'fundamental principle' would not have legal consequences on the other provisions of chapter V of the Convention (A/58/422/Add.1, para. 48), Article 51 is a statement of intent indicating that any doubt concerning the interpretation of provisions related to asset recovery should be resolved in favour of recovery as a core international cooperation objective of the Convention' (p.191).

15 The convention includes provisions for direct recovery of property (art. 53) and international cooperation for purposes of confiscation (art. 54 and 55).

The UNCAC offers no satisfying answer to those questions, and neither does the StAR initiative[16] basically useless under such circumstances. In order to meet this challenge, states who are harbouring stolen assets must implement policies on par with the problem.[17]

However, the inertia of the victim states often combines with similar behaviours from receiving states. Indeed, and despite the various declarations made recently by state representatives during the Pittsburgh (June 2009), Toronto (June 2010) and Seoul (November 2010) G20 summits, it is clear that most states lack the required political will.[18]

How can one explain that no legal action has been taken by the American enforcement authorities against Teodorin Obiang, the son and potential successor to Equatorial Guinea's long-ruling dictator, in spite of the well-publicised and widely known information about its money laundering activities on US soil?[19]

16 StAR is a joint initiative of the WB and UNODC launched in 2007 to facilitate more systematic and timely return of stolen assets. More information available at: http://www1.worldbank.org/publicsector/star_site.

17 StAR agents admitted to their own excessive optimism for having expected numerous requests for assistance from victim states: See StAR, Work Plan (November 24, 2008). Publication available at: http://www1.worldbank.org/publicsector/star_site/documents/about/StAR_Workplan_and Budget_Cover_Note.pdf.

18 In this regard, one can only regret the lack of ambition of the recent RIAA, which will only apply should a request for MLA from a victim country prove itself ineffective. An English version is available at: http://www.assetsearchblog.com/uploads/file/RIAA%283%29.pdf. For a legal commentary of the bill, see M. Perdriel-Vaissière, *La restitution des avoirs illicites – Le cas des Etats défaillants : Les enseignements tirés de l'affaire Mobutu et le projet de loi suisse sur la restitution des valeurs patrimoniales d'origine illicite des personnes politiquement exposées in Garantir que le crime ne paie pas*, Presses Universitaires de Strasbourg (2010).

19 *U.S. Government Documents Crime Spree by Dictator's Son: Why no action by the feds?* By Ken Silverstein, Harpers Magazine (November 2009). Article available at: http://harpers.org/archive/2009/11/hbc-90006022.

Such an attitude, however, is not isolated. One has only to consider the Public Prosecutor's stance in the case known in France as the *Biens Mal Acquis* (literally, ill-gotten gains).[20]

Do we need to remind the reader that according to Article 5 of the OECD Anti-Bribery Convention, '[i]nvestigation and prosecution of the bribery of a foreign public official (...) shall not be influenced by considerations of national economic interest, the potential effect upon relations with another State or the identity of the natural or legal persons involved'?

The ongoing war against transnational corruption has numerous geopolitical implications[21] which constitute serious obstacles to legal action.[22]

Given this, and unless one considers Article 51 of the UNCAC to be mere empty talks, it is crucial that NSAs be able to act when state actors decline to, especially in cases that appear to have been ignored or terminated for political reasons (I). Likewise, NSAs should be allowed to engage in civil proceedings whenever criminal justice is not available (II).[23]

20 The French public prosecutor made several attempts to close down a sovereign corruption case while a preliminary probe substantiated it. More information on that case hereafter.

21 On that topic, see: M. Segonds, *L'internationalisation de l'incrimination de la corruption (...ou le devenir répressif d'une arme économique)*, Droit pénal n° 9, Septembre 2006, Etude 12 ; Juliette Lelieur, La loi du 13 novembre 2007 relative à la lutte contre la corruption : quelles avancées du droit français par rapport aux exigences du droit international ? Droit pénal n° 11, Novembre 2008, étude 25.

22 See Ivan Pavletic, *The Political Economy of Asset Recovery Processes*, International Centre for Asset Recovery (2009).

23 The below comments will focus on the legal remedies and tools that might be used by civil society actors (citizens/NGOs) to address transnational corruption and ensure direct recovery of stolen assets or their confiscation. Legal actions taken by creditors are beyond the scope of this comment.

I. How can NSAs play a role in ensuring that patrimonicide does not pay?

Criminal forfeiture can only take place as part of sentencing following conviction during trial. Knowing that prosecutors usually enjoy discretion in relation to the prosecution of criminal offences, what can NSA do to prevent the offenders from benefiting from the proceeds of their crime?[24]

Apart from the right of private prosecution – mainly available in civil law countries[25] – (B), most legal systems offer alternatives to prosecutorial discretion (A).

Alternatives to prosecutorial discretion

Two methods of limiting or controlling prosecutorial discretion may be available: (1) the law can impose a duty to prosecute, or (2) the prosecutor's refusal to bring charges can be subject to judicial review.

(1) Duty to prosecute: Towards a systematic public enforcement of asset recovery cases

In some legal systems, the prosecutor cannot legally decline to prosecute a case in which, given the evidence available, conviction appears likely. The principle of 'mandatory' prosecution seeks to ensure the equal application of criminal law by mandating its full enforcement. The law denies the prosecutor authority to make exceptions in indi-

24 The following comments are based on the assumptions that cases are brought in the country where stolen assets are located knowing that countries that have ratified UNCAC are required to criminalize the laundering of the proceeds of crime (Art. 23).

25 In the English common law system, private prosecution is theoretically conceivable. However, since England is based on the adversarial system, in practice, only a minuscule portion of prosecutions is actually brought by private citizens because they typically lack the financial means and legal expertise necessary to launch successful prosecutions.

vidual cases, thus precluding favouritism or considerations of political partisanship.

Such a principle applies for example in Spain,[26] Italy[27] and also in Germany, but only with respect to serious felonies.[28]

The duty to prosecute principle could constitute a powerful legal weapon in asset recovery cases.

Provided that NSAs manage to gather sufficient evidence,[29] they could then bring it to the attention of the public prosecutor and/or increase media attention to force the prosecutor to comply with its duty to prosecute.

(2) Judicial review

In most legal systems, it is also possible to request an external review of a prosecutor's ruling. German law for example gives a victim who has reported the offence to the police the right to appeal to the appellate court when the prosecutor has declined prosecution on evidentiary grounds. If the court finds, on the basis of the victim's brief and the prosecutor's file, that sufficient grounds for prosecution exist, it orders the prosecutor to bring charges.[30]

Such a review is also available in England. Two British NGOs in the BAE case recently used this legal recourse. The case involved allegations that the company BAE Systems facilitated the payment of millions of pounds in bribes to senior Saudi officials in order to secure

26 Spanish *Ley de Enjuiciamiento Criminal* – LEC, art.105.

27 *Constituzione della Repubblica italiana, approvata dall'Assemblea Costituente il 22 dic. 1947*, art. 112; Italian *Codice di Procedura Penale*, art. 50.

28 *Strafprozessordnung* – StPO, § 152 sec. 2, § 160.

29 In this regard, Wikileaks.org obviously constitutes a large source of information. For example, thanks to Wikileaks.org, the Kroll Report was made available to the public in 2007. The report was commissioned by Kenyan President Mwai Kibaki in 2002 to investigate and trace assets obtained by President Moi and his close associates by the Goldenberg affair as well as general corruption during his presidency. The report alleges that Mr Moi and associates have obtained amounts adding up to near USD 2 billion. It provided detailed financial records and accounts and shows that Mr Moi made investments in many countries, including property in Australia, South Africa, the United Kingdom, and the United States.

30 *Strafprozessordnung* – StPO, § 171–175 and 395, 1

signing of Al-Yamamah, a GBP 40 billion arms contract between BAE Systems and Saudi Arabia.[31]

In December 2006, the SFO dropped its investigation after its director, Robert Wardle, decided that carrying on could hurt Britain's national security.

On 18 April 2007, two British NGOs, Corner House and CAAT, filed a request at the High Court to call for a judicial review of the SFO's decision. In their application, Corner House and CAAT argued that the decision was unlawful because, as a signatory of the 1997 OECD Anti-Bribery Convention, Britain had a duty to investigate allegations of corruption, even if national security was at risk.

On 10 April 2008, Lord Justice Moses and Mr Justice Sullivan ruled that the decision of the Director of the SFO to drop an investigation into alleged bribes by BAE Systems in Saudi Arabia was unlawful.

Even though that ruling was later overturned by the House of Lords (UK's highest court), it illustrates opportunities that may be available to challenge a prosecutor's ruling.

Combined with media pressure, those tools (i.e. the principle of 'mandatory' prosecution and the judicial review) can play an active role in checking on the public prosecutor's inaction. Another tool for non-state actors, even more efficient, would consist in bringing criminal charges.

Private prosecution

In most civil law systems, private parties are given the right to file criminal charges directly with the court.

Even though Spanish law offers the most far-reaching provision, since Article 125 of the Spanish constitution guarantees every citizen the right to bring criminal charges (2), Article 2 of the French criminal code offers the possibility for the victims to seek damages before the

31 More information about the case available at: http://www.thecornerhouse.org.uk/resources/results/taxonomy:90.

criminal court (1).[32] Those two forms of private prosecution were recently used by NSAs to call for criminal investigations over stolen assets.

(1) The French model: The partie civile mechanism

In French law, victims can launch criminal proceedings by filing a private complaint before an investigating magistrate.[33] That mechanism has been recently used by French NGOs in the BMA case mentioned above.

In March 2007, several French NGOs lodged a criminal complaint before the Public Prosecutor in Paris against the ruling families of Congo-Brazzaville, Equatorial Guinea and Gabon; they alleged that those ruling families owned millions of Euros worth of properties in France that could not be the fruits of their own official salaries.[34] The complaint relied on the charges of concealment of embezzled public funds as provided for by Articles 321-1 and 432-15 of the French Criminal Code. According to those texts, anyone who maintains assets on French soil that were acquired through the commission of an offence (i.e., embezzlement) is punishable by law, no matter where the principal offence took place.

32 According to Article 2 al.1 of the French Code of Criminal Procedure: 'Civil action aimed at the reparation of the damage suffered because of a felony, a misdemeanor or a petty offence is open to all those who have personally suffered damage directly caused by the offence.'

33 However, since 2007, victims seeking to file a criminal case via the *partie civile* mechanism are required to first address the public prosecutor and not the investigating magistrate. This new requirement is provided for by Article 85 of Code of Criminal Procedure: '(…) the civil party petition is admissible only provided that the plaintiff proves that either the public prosecutor let him know, following a complaint lodged before him or a police service, that he will not initiate proceedings, or a three months period has passed by since he lodged the complaint before this magistrate (...).'

34 The complaint was mainly based on the results of an investigative report issued by a report French NGO: *Stolen Assets-Dictators' Wealth and Western connivance* (2007). This report used public data to list and estimate the volume of stolen assets located in Western countries. An updated version of this report is available at: http://ccfd-terresolidaire.org/BMA/.

In June 2007, a police investigation was ordered in response to the complaint. It confirmed most of the allegations and further uncovered tens of millions of euros worth of luxury properties, cars and hundreds of bank accounts belonging to the heads of state from those countries, their family members and close associates. The probe also shed light on the extremely unusual nature of some financing methods. For example, Edith Bongo, the then spouse of the President of Gabon, allegedly acquired a Daimler Chrysler car with a direct money transfer from the Gabonese public treasury.

Despite those findings, the case was closed down in November 2007 after the public prosecutor ruled, in accordance with the principle of opportunity[35] – which governs the French criminal system – that the crimes were 'insufficiently substantiated'.

As a consequence, on 2 December 2008, TI France and Gregory Mintsa, a Gabonese citizen, lodged a criminal complaint via the *partie civile* mechanism before the Dean of investigating magistrates.[36] The objective was to get an investigating magistrate to resume and extend the initial police investigation.

Even before assessing the merits of the case, the magistrate had to rule whether TI France and the Gabonese citizen were allowed to lodge this complaint. In other words, did they have legal standing to sue in this corruption case?[37]

After months of debate opposing the plaintiffs to the Public Prosecutor, the Dean of investigating magistrates ruled on 5 May 2009 that the case lodged by TI France was admissible.[38] This decision was a major contribution to advancing the fight against corruption since,

35 The opportunity principle means that the prosecutors' decision to prosecute or not is discretionary which allows them to take in account factors other than evidence in making their decision. That prosecution system is opposed to those applying the principle of 'mandatory prosecution'.

36 See footnote 32.

37 We will further discuss this question (See part II).

38 The complaint lodged by Gregory Ngbwa Mintsa was dismissed and for security reasons, he renounced to appeal against this decision.

for the first time in France, the collective action of an anti-corruption association was deemed admissible before a criminal court.[39]

The Prosecution office however, appealed the ruling[40] and on 29 October 2009, the Paris Court of Appeal overturned the Dean's decision.[41] TI France lodged an appeal before the *Cour de Cassation* (the Highest court in France) which on 7 November 2010 ruled the case admissible.[42]

As a consequence, three and a half years after the lodging of the initial complaint, two investigating magistrates were designated. They are currently resuming the initial police investigation.

39 This decision was widely commented in French legal reviews : See F. Rome, *Cousu de fil blanc*: Dalloz 2009 p. 1265; G. Roujou de Boubée, *Compétence française pour des détournements de fonds publics commis au préjudice d'Etats africains*: Dalloz 2009 n°22; Ch. Cutajar, *L'affaire des «biens mal acquis» ou le droit pour la société civile de contribuer judiciairement à la lutte contre la corruption*: JCP Edition Générale n° 22, 27 Mai 2009, act. 277.

40 It is also worth noting that the Public Prosecutor's attempts to prevent the case from being pursued led to the question being discussed by the National Assembly. On 12 May 2009, during a routine session of questions to the government, a Socialist member of parliament formally asked the Minister of Justice Rachida Dati whether the Ministry or any other state body had exerted any influence over the Office of Public Prosecution (complete records of this exchange can be accessed at: http://www.assemblee-nationale.fr/13/cri/2008-2009/20090238.asp).

41 See Ch. Cutajar, *Affaire «des biens mal acquis», un arrêt qui ne clôt pas le débat*: JCP Edition Générale n° 51, 14 Décembre 2009, p.563; C. Cutajar et M. Perdriel-Vaissière, *Réforme de la procédure pénale: l'action citoyenne, nouvel outil de lutte contre la corruption transnationale?*, Dalloz 2010 p.1295.

42 F. Rome, *Noirs délires...*, Dalloz 2010 p. 2641; G. Roujou de Boubée, *Affaire dite des «biens mal acquis» (suite)*, Dalloz 2010 p. 2760 ; S. Lavric, *Affaire des «biens mal acquis»: recevabilité de la constitution de partie civile de l'association Transparence International France*, Dalloz 2010, act. 2707; C. Cutajar, *Affaire des biens mal acquis: la chambre criminelle ordonne le retour de la procédure au juge d'instruction*, JCP Edition Générale n° 48, 29 Novembre 2010, p. 1174; M. Perdriel-Vaissière, *La poursuite des faits de corruption à la lumière de l'affaire des Biens Mal Acquis*, Dalloz 2011 p. 112.

(2) The Spanish model: the acción popular

According to Spanish criminal law, any Spanish citizen or NGO can bring a criminal action (*querella*) before an investigating magistrate.[43] Contrary to the French *partie civile* mechanism, the petitioner does not need to demonstrate having suffered a prejudice to be entitled to act.[44] Upon receiving a citizen's complaint, the investigating magistrate is obliged to conduct a preliminary investigation unless the facts in question do not constitute an offence.[45]

The *acción popular* can play a vital role in asset recovery, as illustrated by a recent case brought by a Spanish NGO with support from OSJI.[46]

On 22 October 2008, APDHE filed a criminal complaint before the Dean of investigating magistrates (*El Juzgado Central de Instrucción*) alleging that eleven family members and close associates of the President of Equatorial Guinea were diverting large amounts of the country's oil revenues to purchase real estate in Spain – facts that constitute the offence of money laundering.[47]

The Spanish case was built on extensive investigations and hearings conducted several years before by the Permanent Subcommittee on Investigations of the US Senate Committee on Governmental Affairs, which had documented suspicious transactions between the offi-

43 *Ley de Enjuiciamiento Criminal* – LEC, Articles 101 and 270.

44 Some individuals, however, are not entitled to *acción popular* (See *Ley de Enjuiciamiento Criminal* – LEC, Article 102).

45 *Ley de Enjuiciamiento Criminal* – LEC, art. 637.

46 More information about the case available at: http://www.soros.org/initiatives/justice/litigation/obiangfamily.

47 The Spanish Criminal Code makes it a crime for anyone to acquire, convert or transfer property knowing that such property was purchased by the proceeds from a serious crime, or for anyone to perform any other act to conceal or disguise its unlawful origin or to aid another person who has participated in the crime in evading the legal consequence of the crime. The defendants in this case regularly diverted funds from the Equatoguinean Treasury by ordering Riggs Bank to make the various transfers to private accounts held by a shell company controlled by the defendants and the President of Equatorial Guinea. The fact that the embezzlement may have been committed abroad is irrelevant because the Spanish Penal Code grants jurisdiction to Spanish courts over money laundering cases occurring in Spain, regardless of where the underlying crime occurred.

cial Equatoguinean governmental oil revenues account maintained at the US-based Riggs Bank, and a private account maintained at Banco Santander in Spain, by a company believed to be owned in whole or in part by President Obiang.[48] Further investigations undertaken by OSJI and APDHE revealed close correlations in timing between several of the bank transfers and real estate purchases throughout Spain on behalf of the president, his family, and close associates.

The case was ruled admissible and a criminal investigation is currently underway in the Pre-Trial Investigative Court in Las Palmas, where the money at issue was allegedly received.

These two cases illustrate the potential of using private prosecution to enhance asset recovery: provided that private parties manage to collect sufficient evidence from which it appears likely that an offence has been committed,[49] they can bypass the public prosecutor's inaction and bring forth a criminal complaint.

***

The various above-mentioned cases indicate the various ways by which NSAs can push for law enforcement and ensure that crime does not pay. However, there are situations where criminal justice is not available either because the accused have died, have absconded or cannot be prosecuted for reasons of immunity.[50]

In such cases, civil proceedings become particularly attractive to apply for damages and/or the recovery of stolen property.

48 *Money laundering and foreign corruption: enforcement and effectiveness of the Patriot Act*, United States Senate Permanent Subcommittee on Investigations, Committee on Governmental Affairs, July 2004. Report available at: http://hsgac.senate.gov/public/_files/ACF5F8.pdf.

49 Criminal procedure in most civil law countries is inquisitorial which makes things easier for private parties to lodge criminal complaints as long as charges appear likely.

50 Criminal proceedings are aimed at sentencing a defendant for a violation of the law. To be prosecuted, the latter must be personally liable (Action *in personam*). In other words, any event affecting the defendant's liability (death, immunity) prevents prosecution. Standards of proof might also preclude a criminal conviction. For instance, if the evidence is unlikely to establish a criminal conviction beyond a reasonable doubt, it is also unlikely to result in a criminal confiscation.

II. How can NSAs play a role in ensuring redress for victims?

According to Article 35 of the UNCAC, any person or entity having suffered damage 'as a result of an act of corruption [should] have the right to initiate legal proceedings against those responsible for that damage in order to obtain compensation'.

To what extent can this provision support NSAs claims seeking the recovery of assets allegedly misappropriated through criminal activity?

If and when victim status cannot be usefully invoked (A), NSAs should be allowed to sue on behalf of the victim state (B).[51]

Ordinary civil litigation & the status of victims

Patrimonicide is not a victimless crime; the ultimate victims of acts of indigenous spoliation are ordinary citizens. And yet, as illustrated by the BMA case, the *locus standi* requirement constitutes a real obstacle to ordinary civil litigation by private parties (1). In any case, the rules on the repartition of the prejudice offer no guarantee regarding stolen asset recovery (2).

(1) The standing issue obstacle

According to the legal standing requirement applicable in most jurisdictions (also known as the *locus standi*), parties can only sue when they have an interest at stake and for damage that they have personally suffered. In other words, only the affected parties have the *locus standi* to file a case and pursue the litigation while non-affected persons have no *locus standi* to do so.

Locus standi is an admissibility condition that acts as a gatekeeper for the filing of cases. If a complainant does not have standing,

51 The following comments are based on the assumptions that claims are brought in the country where stolen assets are located knowing that most foreign jurisdictions are competent to hear civil proceedings if the stolen assets are located within its territory.

it will be rejected by the judicial body on formal grounds, without consideration of the merits of the case.

When dealing with grand corruption, the primary victims are states but it is also clear that citizens suffer damage as a result of the mismanagement of public resources.[52] However, citizens are rarely considered as victims, and thus legally entitled to initiate civil proceedings and apply for damages.

In the French BMA case, Gregory Mintsa and TI France had attempted to prove having suffered a prejudice, a *sine qua non* condition for effective prosecution as specified by Article 2 of the French Criminal Code of Procedure.[53] According to its text, in order to be ruled admissible, the prejudice must be both direct and personal:

- The prejudice must be direct, which means that there must be a causal connection between the injury and the offence;
- The prejudice must be personal, which means that by its very nature, the offence is susceptible to cause a prejudice to an individual or entity. In France, prior to 1992, corruption was ranked as an offence against the public interest (i.e., the issues at stake regard matters of public interest) for which only the Public Prosecutor was allowed to prosecute. Since a major decision (Cass. crim., 1er dec. 1992), it is now admitted that corruption issues can overlap with private interests. From that point on, private parties were allowed to bring criminal charges in corruption matters. This jurisprudence is so well-established in French law that the Public Prosecutor did not even try to dispute the personal nature of the prejudice invoked by the complainants in the BMA case.

In the end, the whole discussion focused on the existence of a causal connection between the presence of alleged stolen assets in French territory and the prejudice alleged by Gregory Mintsa and TI France.

52 See C. Cutajar, *Le droit à réparation des victimes de la corruption: Plaidoyer pour la reconnaissance d'un statut des victimes de la corruption*, Dalloz 2008, n° 16.

53 Although the following developments are described within the context of criminal procedure, the associated principles are transposable to civil action.

With respect to Gregory Mintsa, it was argued that, as a tax payer, he should be entitled to question the way his money is being used, and allowed to sue whoever mismanaged public assets. He must be considered as a victim since his taxes were allocated to the personal enrichment of the inner circle of the President of Gabon instead of being allotted to the whole community; from which he suffered direct prejudice.

The investigating magistrate, who ruled that Gregory Mintsa had no standing, rejected this reasoning, arguing that only the Gabonese state was entitled to the status of victim under such circumstances. This ruling came as no surprise, as there was no legal ground or judicial precedent to endorse such a claim.[54]

As for TI France, things went on differently. In French Law, an association is allowed to initiate proceedings to defend collective interests provided that it is formally authorised to do so.[55] Associations fighting corruption do not benefit from such an authorisation. However, on the basis of Article 2 of the Criminal Code f Procedure, jurisprudence has admitted, in some cases, that a non-legally entitled association could be ruled admissible as soon as the offence directly impairs the collective interests the association assigned itself to defend.[56] In other words, there must be an exact correspondence between the purpose and mission of TI France and the facts in question.

Based on that jurisprudence, it was argued that the facts denounced in the criminal complaint fell directly under TI France's object, which is precisely to fight corruption. The embezzlement of public assets by corrupt rulers and their subsequent retaining on French

54 The solution would have been identical had the case been of strictly local scope: 'A civil claim brought by a communal taxpayer against the mayor over alleged embezzlement and corruption acts which he claims would cause him a prejudice due to increased local taxes is inadmissible' (Cass. crim., 25 oct. 1934 :Bull. crim. 1934, n° 169).

55 Articles 2-1 to 2-21 of the Criminal Code of Procedure provide the list of associations allowed to initiate legal action for the defense of their collective interests.

56 Previous examples include the associations opposing tobacco use (Cass. crim. 7 février 1984: Bull. crim. n° 41; Cass. crim. 29 avril 1986: Bull. crim n° 146), honouring the memory of World War II deportees (Cass. Crim 14 janvier 1971: Bull. crim n°14), or more recently, associations for the protection of the environment (Cass. crim. 12 septembre 2006 : Bull. crim. n° 217).

soil were directly against the actions carried out by the association since its creation.

As seen before, the *Cour de Cassation* eventually ruled that TI France had a standing to sue.

This decision constitutes a milestone since it makes possible first prosecution, then criminal confiscation of the illegal assets; however, we must ask ourselves what the impact of such a decision would have been, had it been made by a civil court.

(2) Rules applicable to compensation

The main purpose of civil justice is to compensate the victims for the prejudice they suffered. This reparation can operate in kind or in value (by payment of damages) but at any rate the reparation amount paid to the victim cannot exceed the actual prejudice said victim has suffered. As such, assuming TI France and/or the Gabonese citizen would have been able to ascertain their standing to sue before civil courts, and assuming the civil responsibility of the defendants could have been established, neither plaintiffs could have claimed a right to the restitution of the stolen assets.[57]

In the final analysis, the only way to guarantee the restitution of illegal assets to victim populations is to allow the NSAs to act in the name and on behalf of the despoiled state.

The potential of Public Interest Litigation (PIL)[58] in asset recovery

As a legal tool capable of seeking redress on matters affecting the public interest (A), PIL has a vital role to play in ensuring the repatriation of looted assets to victim states (B).

57 In the case of associations' prejudice, the judges usually compensate associations with the payment of a single symbolic Euro. As for Gregory, such a hypothesis would have required from the judges a quite surreal casuistry.

58 It is also called public law litigation or strategic litigation.

(1) Seeking redress on matters affecting the public interest

According to Black's Law Dictionary, PIL is a legal action initiated in a court of law for the enforcement of public interest or general interest and in which the public or class of the community have a pecuniary interest, or some interest, by which their legal rights or liabilities are affected.[59]

PIL claims are based on relaxed rules of standing. Individuals and groups who want to bring cases to a court of law on matters affecting the public interest are allowed standing even though they do not have a real and personal interest in the matter.

One usually distinguishes two kinds of PIL claims.

On one hand, PIL claims can be aimed at bringing about social change. In that context, PIL is used to achieve long and short-term ends: to raise public awareness, mobilise constituencies, gain political leverage, and to develop a culture of accountability and norms of legality, irrespective of victory or defeat in courts.[60]

On the other hand, PIL claims can be aimed at seeking to redress on matters affecting the public interest. In that context, PIL is a right given to a socially conscious member or a public spirited NGO to espouse a public cause by seeking judicial action for the redress of public injury.[61]

India, for instance, has been a pioneer in PIL, but one can find provisions empowering disinterested citizen action in numerous legal systems.

In France, for example, any taxpayer[62] has the right to take action and substitute himself/herself to the local community (city, county, state) in order to claim compensation for any prejudice suffered by said community.[63]

59 Black's Law Dictionary, (7th edition) 1229, 1990

60 See J. Lobel, *Losers, Fools & Prophets: Justice as Struggle*, 80 Cornell L (1995).

61 On the differences between PIL and Class Actions, see B.A Levine, Defending the Public Interest: Citizen Suits for Restitution Against Bribed Officials, 48 Tenn. L. Rev. 347 (Winter, 1981).

62 It is worth noting that the state-level taxpayer doesn't enjoy such a capacity; neither do foreign taxpayers.

63 This mechanism had allowed legal action against Jacques Chirac in the case of the Mairie de Paris' fictive jobs.

Likewise, some jurisdictions in the US empower citizens with the right to institute civil proceedings on behalf of the community in matters of public corruption.[64]

In many jurisdictions, commercial laws provide that any shareholder can bring a civil suit on behalf of the company whenever the company refuses to take up legal action: this is called the *ut singuli* action or shareholders' derivate suits.[65] The shareholders are not suing for their own interests as individuals, but are instead suing on behalf of the interests of the whole company; thus, any monetary compensation is due to the company.

Those mechanisms are essentially limited to matters within the domestic jurisdiction of a state. However, wouldn't it be possible to transpose those principles and solutions to asset recovery procedures of transnational scope?

(2) Repatriation of looted assets through Public Interest Litigation (PIL)

In the above-mentioned BMA case, the plaintiffs had attempted to establish Gregory Mintsa's entitlement to the *partie civile* status by arguing that, as a Gabonese citizen, he should have the right to take judicial action in the name and on behalf of the Gabonese state. The judges had dismissed this argument: they considered that the lack of any explicit provision entitling him to act led to his complaint not being admissible in court.

This view is regrettable; equity would command to favour a flexible interpretation of legal rules each and every time their strict enforcement would have unfair or unreasonable consequences; this was clearly one of those cases.

NSAs (citizens and/or NGOs) should be allowed to bring civil claims on behalf of victim states to seek restitution of stolen wealth.[66]

64 See B.A Levine, Defending the Public Interest: Citizen Suits for Restitution Against Bribed Officials, 48 Tenn. L. Rev. 347 (Winter, 1981)

65 Often, this kind of legal matter involves the actions done or performed by the corporation's executives.

66 PIL could also apply to civil forfeiture (non-conviction based forfeiture) whenever available.

Courts should recognize that a bona fide litigant with neither an arguable case, which is not vexatious, frivolous, nor an abuse of the process of the court ought not to be denied standing.

III. Conclusion

According to StAR, of the hundreds of billions of dollars stolen over the course of the last fifteen years, no more than USD 5 billion have been recovered.[67] This is equivalent to the amount reportedly stolen by Mobutu Sese Seko.[68]

NSAs have a vital role to play to improve this result and enable effective asset recovery to take place. Whenever possible, NSAs should take legal actions to get stolen assets confiscated or to ensure proper compensation of the victim countries.

Such an involvement of NSAs might also have a powerful deterrent effect: if private parties can hold public officials accountable, acts of indigenous spoliation might become less widespread, and officers might perform their fiduciary duties to the public in a more wholesome fashion.

Litigation however is costly and there is a crucial need for the international development community to support private litigation and finally to turn Article 51 into reality.

67 *Stolen Asset Recovery: Toward a Global Architecture for Asset Recovery*, The World Bank and the United Nations Office of Drugs and Crimes (UNODC), 2008. Report available at: http://siteresources.worldbank.org/EXTSARI/Resources/5570284125717205 2492/GlobalArchitectureFinalwithCover.pdf?resourceurlname=GlobalArchitectureFinalwithCover.pdf.

68 Global Study on the Transfer of Funds of Illicit Origin, Especially Funds Derived from Acts of Corruption, UN General Assembly, November 2002. Report available at: http://www.unodc.org/pdf/crime/convention_corruption/session_4/12f.pdf.

MICHEAL LEVI AND NICHOLAS LORD

Links between corruption and organised crime and research gaps

I. Introduction

Organised crime is a term that is often used quite carelessly, but carries with it the image of The Godfather and criminal hierarchies that sometimes corrupt police and politicians, usually involved in extortion, vice and/or drugs trafficking. Legally, anything between the Camorra, on the one hand and, on the other hand, three burglars, a window cleaning business and a foreign bank account can meet the criteria for 'transnational organised crime' of the UNTOC, though national implementing legislation is quite varied in how organised crime or mafia-type associations are defined, even within the EU. In addition to these, there is a great deal of discretion in what sorts of activities and groups/networks that potentially are definable as 'organised crime' are focused upon.

It is a common misconception that 'organised crime' applies only to *per se* illegal activities such as drugs trafficking: any criminal activities can in principle be the basis for the label. Thus one might define as organised crime an alliance between corrupt leaders (elected or not), family members and others (perhaps including the police or military) to embezzle funds from national treasuries or even to extract monopoly profits from superficially legal businesses, provided that they can violate some criminal law in doing so. If banks can be shown to be knowingly laundering the proceeds of such activities, they too become part of 'organised crime'. Whether there is a realistic chance of prosecution is a separate question: where investigators, prosecutors and/or judges have no genuine independence from the *de facto* or *de jure* state, or where crucial evidence is unobtainable from the same or other jurisdictions, then court outcomes are unfeasible (and the use of the term may be defamatory). The concept of organised crime itself produces the wrong analytical question, 'which is to ask if 'it' is organized in a particular way, whereas the more sensible question is to ask what factors over time shape the ways in which crimes of certain types are organized and who [beyond just the perpetrators] gets involved in them?' (Levi, 2007: 779). Below is a high-level abstraction of the process involved.

Box 1 *The organisation of crime: a process model*

- See a situation as a 'crime' or 'profit-generating' opportunity.
- Obtain whatever finance is needed for the crime.
- Find people willing and able to offend (if this is necessary for the crime contemplated) and who are controllable and reliable.
- Obtain any chemical precursors/equipment/data needed to offend.
- Carry out offences in domestic and/or overseas locations with or without physical presence in jurisdiction(s).
- Minimise immediate enforcement/operational risks. Especially if planning to repeat crimes, neutralise law enforcement by technical skill, by corruption, and/or by legal arbitrage, using legal obstacles to enforcement operations and prosecutions which vary between jurisdictions.
- Convert, where necessary, the fruits of crime into money or other usable assets in desired currencies.
- Spend as much of the proceeds as you want – a flexible phenomenon which may change over time.
- Find people and places willing to store those proceeds you wish to retain (and perhaps conceal their origin – i.e. launder the funds).
- Decide which jurisdiction(s) offers the optimal balance between social/physical comfort and the risk of asset forfeiture/criminal justice sanctions. This may vary over time. Indifference in any one state or sub-state arena may suffice to neutralise an investigation, and staffing inadequacies as well as corruption may be the cause of official inaction.

The set of skills that are needed depend on the type of crime that is contemplated, and there can be variation in the order in which they are arranged, some being more pre-planned than others. One typology of crimes is as follows, adapted from Naylor (2003):

Box 2 *A typology of profit-driven crimes*

- Predatory – e.g., burglary, robbery
- Commercial – the use of businesses as fronts to commit crimes; cartels
- Market Based (including trafficking)
  - *Regulations* (conditional contraband) – e.g., evasion of controls on arms sales
  - *Taxes* (fiscal contraband) – e.g., smuggling licitly produced tobacco, transfer pricing
  - *Prohibitions* (absolute contraband) – principally drugs trafficking

Market offences (e.g. illegal drugs trafficking) may be and sometimes identifiably are committed by the same people who steal and defraud, but offenders and offence levels react differently to crime control. Total prevention of smuggling is inconceivable, but what is important for present purposes is how concentrated the market is, and how far up the chain corruption of officials reaches in order to permit the criminal activities to continue. It should be stressed that even in societies where there is grand corruption, what economists call 'rent-seeking'[1] by lower down personnel may be permitted as part of the tacit exchange of benefits: police and other public officials may be licensed to steal, partly to encourage loyalty and a stake in 'the system'.

Some research issues that we will be examining here, fairly briefly, are:

1. What do we know about how crimes are organised and the relationship between this and different forms of corruption;

1 Rent-seeking occurs when an individual (high or low in formal status) or organisation seeks to earn income by capturing funds through manipulation or exploitation of the economic or political environment, instead of earning profits through competitive economic transactions and the production of added wealth. It can be an issue of dispute whether benefits are 'rent' or legitimate profit.

2. Measuring costs, prevalence and incidence, including saving/laundering the proceeds internally and externally;
3. Criminal justice controls – what do we know about how they work and their impacts on convictions/confiscation success, and deterrence/incapacitation/public satisfaction
4. Non-criminal justice controls such as civil forfeiture, trading bans, and their impacts.

II. The organisation of serious crimes, and its linkage with corruption

Whether hierarchically or more flexibly organised, crime networks who want to transfer untaxed legal or illegal commodities (drugs and people) across borders and within countries unmolested may decide that corruption is a necessary business cost. Bribery, considered the most common instrument of corruption, involves two willing actors, and can therefore be active (giving/offering) or passive (receiving/soliciting), though it may also involve extortionate demands by those in a position to produce significant benefits and/or sanctions. Bribes may involve cash payoffs, hospitalities/gifts, and non-monetary favours such as various services, amongst others, and can be intended to speed up otherwise lawful acts or acts prohibited in an official's course of duty. Often there are no direct victims in the commonly understood sense of that term. In some societies where there is a high expectation that bribes will be welcome, this is easy, and there may exist semi-official routines that filter pay-offs upwards and perhaps downwards, depending on the country and time. In other countries, expectations of bribability may be very low, and secure lines of illicit product delivery may have to depend on skill at covert behaviour. (Though the supply of drugs and vice is slower and less efficient if other people do not know these services are available.) There is no automatic correspondence between (a) elite corruption in contracts with otherwise lawful government departments (e.g., defence) and with importers/exporters or extractive industries, and (b) elite or non-elite involvement in corruption in wholly illicit trades such as drugs and people trafficking. However in highly concentrated societies, these may be inter-correlated, even if only in 'trickle up' from (b). Some elites have a predatory attitude, searching actively for rent-generating opportunities: the Marcos, Suharto and – allegedly – Ben Ali families are good examples of this.

Definitions of 'organised crime' often include corruption as central to it, largely because of the commercial benefits of ensuring a smooth supply of vice (Fickenauer, 2005: 65; Hagan, 2006: 129). Prosecutors and investigators disagree as to how essential it is for organised crime to be able to corrupt officials: some see it as critical; others see it as exaggerated (Beare, 1997: 158). Furthermore, some serious crimes such as complex frauds may not rely on or involve corruption at all (Maltz, 1994: 27): such predatory activities do not have to operate out in the open as crimes in the way that some sellers of illegal drugs do. However, empirical analyses of the links between corruption and organised crime are limited. A recent report for the European Commission from the CSD (2010: 33) outlined that the lack of specific studies in the EU addressing the links between corruption and organised crime has numerous explanations: first, very few governments study the problem, and of those that do, reports and findings are often not published due to the content being sensitive or self-discrediting; second, academic criminological research is based on police or judicial sources; and third, criminologists in some EU member states are not conducting empirically based research on organised crime, and in other countries, those that do conduct research, conduct it for governmental institutes where the topic of organised crime and corruption is generally not favoured. (See, for an ultra-sceptical approach to organised crime policies, van Duyne, 2010.)

This criminological trend can be seen in the UK where a simple search for the terms 'corruption' and 'organised crime' in the *British Journal of Criminology* from January 2000 to March 2011 returned only 14 articles and of these, none addressed the links between corruption and organised crime as their substantive focus. While some of the articles acknowledged a link or referred to corruption being a key process of organised crime, only one of the articles was of direct relevance to this topic – the role of corruption in relation to cigarette counterfeiting (Shen et al., 2010). This applied to other journals also. However even within the EU, confidential reviews of performance against 'organised crime' have led to public criticism of and financial sanctions against Bulgaria[2] and Romania.[3] These are linked to suspicions of high-level corruption and intentional under-performance against organised crime. Outside the EU, a 2010 Council of Europe report alleged serious involvement in corruption and organised crime of the current (and subsequently re-elected in 2011) Prime Minister of Kosovo.[4]

The modesty of UK research about the relationship between corruption and organised crime is also largely the case throughout Western Europe, although Italy has produced a number of relevant studies (see Ruggiero, 2010; della Porta and Vannucci, 1999; Paoli, 2003). Ruggiero (2010: 103) suggests '[c]orruption and organised crime…are intertwined in a 'criminal system' that reproduces power, be it illicit or otherwise'. His focus on the organised crime-corruption relationship in Italy attempts to delineate the uniqueness of the Italian case though observations around the specific contours of organised and corrupt exchange in the country as they manifest themselves. He concludes that corruption and organised crime are so closely intertwined, that investigations of corruption often involve some criminal organisation and that when investigating organised crime, the involvement of some corrupt politician or entrepreneur often becomes apparent (2010: 102). Conventional analyses suggesting organised crime is mainly responsible for the spreading of corruption do not hold up, however, as Ruggiero's data suggests that in Italy, 'widespread corruption within the social, economic and political spheres attracts organised criminal groups, encouraging them to participate in corrupt exchange and indirectly boosting their other various illicit activities' (2010: 102).

In North America, the links between corruption and organised crime have received significant analysis. Beare (1997: 158) notes that

2 Available at http://ec.europa.eu/dgs/secretariat_general/cvm/docs/com_2011_81_en.pdf.

3 Available at http://ec.europa.eu/dgs/secretariat_general/cvm/docs/com_2011_80_en.pdf.

4 Available at http://www.assembly.coe.int/CommitteeDocs/2010/ajdoc462010prov.pdf.

corruptive actions enable criminals to buy protection from enforcement, eliminate competition and subsequently amass capital. organised crime operations vary in the extent to which they are able to acquire support and assistance through corruption: unsophisticated and unintegrated criminal groups lack this ability, especially when in their embryonic stages. The extent to which an individual or group is well integrated into 'legitimate' society shapes their ability to corrupt. Acquiring influential positions and power, and becoming significantly embedded in the power structure of the economic, political and/or criminal justice sphere, enables organised crime operations to be more easily defined as legitimate. This leads to a degree of invisibility whereby corrupt activities are defined as 'normal' operations of business or enterprise. Thus, the more an organised crime group can corrupt, the more they remain invisible or are seen to be legitimate. Beare (1997: 159) further notes that organised crime activity and/or the actions of corrupt officials can become so deep within a particular society that the reliance of legitimate business or the political regime on corrupted processes causes the society's institutions themselves to become corrupted. One might add to this that even where the criminal investigation team is honest, elite connections within law enforcement or within wider society generate significant risks to enforcement that deter action without particularly strong evidence, for fear of negative 'blowback'.

Looking more globally, Buscaglia and van Dijk (2003) suggest organised crime and corruption in the public sector are shaped by weak control mechanisms of the state and civil society. The results of their statistically based analysis (largely utilising perception studies to develop composite indices) suggest that in countries at all stages of development, levels of organised crime and of corruption in the public sector are primarily shaped by the quality of core public state institutions, such as the police, prosecution and the court. The authors go on to suggest that organised crime and corruption in the public sector are more susceptible than 'conventional' crime to state intervention (2003: 31–32). However, the extent to which statistical analyses can adequately understand the 'quality' of an institution is debatable, while the efficacy of state intervention in a 'captured' public sector, or a public sector with high levels of organised crime and corruption is unclear. A further attempt to address the link between organised crime and corruption through statistical analysis (on often problematic data) is offered by van Dijk (2007). Perception studies and economic surveys along with other statistical sources provide the empirical basis of van Dijk's causal model of the independent effect of organised crime, rule of law, and corruption on national wealth. The findings of his COCI suggest that political strategies tolerating the activities of local criminal groups in order to increase national wealth are unlikely to be successful. Van Dijk concludes that while some forms of organised crime may bring significant revenues, 'tolerating Mafia-type activities implies letting the Trojan horse of racketeering and grand corruption into the walls of government' (2007: 39). However, the extent to which 'Mafia-type' activities reflect the actual criminal activities of organised crime groups or even represent the majority of criminal activity in these areas is debatable. One of the implicit problems is the operationalization of 'organised crime groups' into simple analytical categories, an issue that also applies to many threat assessments.

Europol's (2009) OCTA report developed an organised crime group typology within which the use of and reliance on corruption and corruptive influences and behaviours to interfere with law enforcement and judicial processes defined one particular group (2009: 15). Behaviour in this category uses middle-level corruptive influence against law enforcement to avoid detection or any low or middle level corruptive influence to hinder an ongoing law enforcement or judicial process (2009: 41). The report (2009: 42) also indicates that intelligence gathering on the use of corruption in local societies and economies in third countries is more difficult for EU law enforcement agencies due to a lack of information and possible misinterpretation: first, available information does not enable clear identification of the strategies of organised crime groups outside the EU; second, law enforcement agencies can only observe events that might be interpreted as indicators of corruptive influence by organised crime groups: this includes, for example, difficulties in international co-operation, deficiencies in law enforcement, poor administration; and third, corruption-use in the EU is interpreted as indicating higher levels of corruption outside the EU. These present a number of obstacles to a clear appreciation of the issue. The report indicates member states that have reported having such organised crime groups intending to influence law enforcement include the UK and Ireland in Northern Europe; and Romania, the Slovak Republic, the Czech Republic, Hungary, Poland, Lithuania, and Latvia in Central and Eastern Europe. However, such largely self-report mechanisms under-estimate the problems, the unmentioned Sweden, for example, being shown by research to have a surprisingly high rate of attempts to exert influence on public officials by corruption and threats (Korsell and Skinnari, 2010).

Other studies have addressed the link between organised crime and corruption from a purely economic/theoretical position. Kugler *et al.* (2005), for example, analyse an oligopoly model in which differentiated criminal organisations compete globally on criminal activities and use corruptive practices at the local level to avoid punishment. They conclude that when the cost of bribing is low, increased policing and sanctions generate higher crime rates and that once a punishment threshold is passed, even more crime can follow. These findings are, however, not based on empirical understandings of the phenomena and are located within narrow models of economic rationality.

The Eurobarometer (2006: 11) public opinion survey researches opinions on organised, cross-border crime and corruption and suggests that in the EU, more than half of citizens (54%) believe that most corruption in their country is caused by organised crime, while 35% believe the opposite and 11% have no opinion. The limitations of opinion and perception studies are many and the extent to which opinions reflect actual phenomena is difficult to substantiate. Further studies emanating from the private sector have also acknowledged the link between organised crime and corruption, although not as the substantive focus of their reports, which are primarily on fraud but include corruption and bribery, as well as indicators of organised crime such as money laundering (see PwC's (2007) *Global Economic Crime Survey*; Ernst and Young's (2010) *Global Fraud Survey;* Kroll's (2010/2011) *Global Fraud Report*).

Further literature exists that examines the links between corruption and organised crime in specific analytically distinct areas. The CSD (2010) report separates this literature into eight areas: general studies addressing corruption and organised crime (see Fickenauer, 2005; Hagan, 2006; Beare, 1997); judicial corruption and OC (see della Porta and Vannucci, 1999); political corruption and organised crime (see della Porta and Vannucci, 1999; Godson, 2003); police corruption and organised crime (see Miller, 2003; Van de Bunt, 2004); corruption in the military and organised crime (see Davis *et al.*, 2001); corruption in prisons and organised crime (see for example Edwards (Daily Telegraph), 2008); administrative corruption and organised crime (see Davis *et al.*, 2001; CSD, 2007)); and, private sector corruption (see Albanese, 1995; Jacobs and Peters, 2003; Edelhertz and Overcast, 1993). These diverse areas outline the analytical and conceptual difficulties in talking about corruption and organised crime which abstractions often fail to reflect the diverse types of crimes that fall into these categories, where they occur, who is involved in them and how they are controlled.

A common difficulty therefore with studies that fall into the above global categories is that they render subsequent analysis disconnected and de-contextualised. The analytical focus in such studies on the concept of 'organised crime' is a problem in itself: shifting focus away from abstract notions of 'it' towards developing theories of the organisation of serious crimes (see Edwards and Levi, 2008) enables a more contextual understanding of the social relations and multiple activities that organised crimes or corrupt actions involve. Levi (2007), discussing the organisation of serious crimes, outlines the usefulness of thinking about the tasks that need to be performed to commit serious crimes over a long period. In this way we shift analytical focus towards concrete social practices, processes and relations (see Boxes 1 and 2 earlier.) In examining the gaps in the research between organised crime and corruption, thinking about the above tasks provides a useful starting point in beginning to address the actual relations between corruption and organised crime.

III. How much money laundering is there?

Both corruption and organised crime generate income, and something has to be done with that income. Some of it is simply spent in direct conspicuous consumption; some of it is saved domestically; and some of it is exported to 'offshore finance centres'. There are no systematic data on how many places proceeds of corruption or organised crime travel through, or on final destinations. However although (as recent actions against Ben Ali, Gaddafi and Mubarak in 2011 show) funds and property overtly held in the West can be frozen and perhaps confiscated, rational preferences would be to keep at least part of the funds in safe and discreet countries in the West, rather than in more secret but maybe more volatile havens in the South Pacific, from where the funds might disappear into other hands.

A modern problem requires estimation of its scale, so that it can be compared to other problems and so that performance measures can be developed against which to judge the efforts of those who aim to combat it. Thus there has been a modest line of efforts to develop estimates of money laundering at the national and global levels: see Reuter and Truman (2004, Chapter 2) for a review. It should be understood that whatever our folk images of money laundering are, anything that is done to proceeds of all crimes to conceal or move or transform it counts as laundering: so putting money into one's bank account in one's own name is laundering if the money comes from crime. Thus only proceeds directly consumed are not laundered.

Global data on money laundering (and, for that matter, corruption, fraud and organised crime) are often used merely as advocacy, all reasonable reservations disappearing in the media-fuelled need to produce a very large figure. It is not clear that it is either useful or feasible to estimate the figure. Numbers are frequently cited, with minimal documentation, becoming 'facts by repetition.' For example, the IMF estimated a total of USD 590 billion to USD 1.5 trillion globally in 1996. In 2005 the United Nations cited the range of USD 500 billion to USD 1 trillion.[5] A more recent set of gravity-defying estimates based on problematic assumptions may be found in Walker and Unger (2009). A sustained effort between 1996 and 2000 by the FATF to produce a fully documented estimate failed. There are, however, a few estimates of the potential demand for money laundering that are regularly treated as actual money-laundering estimates. The estimates fall into two categories: macroeconomic and microeconomic. Neither

5 Available at http://www.unodc.org/unodc/en/money_laundering.html.

method yields estimates that can be considered as anything more than indicative. The macroeconomic estimates are methodologically flawed: they generate implausibly high figures. For example, taken at face value they indicate that the German economy grew fifty percent faster than measured officially over the period 1991–2001 (Schneider and Enste, 2000). The microeconomic estimates lack a credible empirical base. For instance, fraud, the largest source of criminal revenues for the US is estimated from a survey that had only a 10 percent response rate and asked questions very imperfectly related to the relevant quantity (Association of Certified Fraud Examiners, 2002; see more generally, Levi et al., 2007). Estimates of drugs expenditure and the profits from drugs sales and how they are distributed remain largely speculative. An absorbing Rand study suggested that Mexican DTOs' gross revenues (significantly more than profit) from moving marijuana across the border into the United States and selling it to wholesalers is likely less than USD 2 billion, and their preferred estimate is closer to USD 1.5 billion; for all drugs, the total gross estimate is USD 5.1 billion (Kilmer et al., 2010: 30), plus relatively modest further income in the low hundreds of millions from people trafficking.[6]

Even taken at face value, these numbers are only weakly related to money laundering. Even Mexican DTOs have large expenses in bribes to law enforcement and politicians; and (as in the case of Irish and other paramilitaries) they have large levels of staffing to support, mainly in cash from cash proceeds of crimes. The dollarization of Mexico means that they do not even have currency conversion problems. In addition to such organised criminal activity, much income from selling drugs is earned by relatively disorganised offenders who use the cash to directly purchase legal goods without making use of any financial institution. Small-time thieves earning USD 25,000 annually are unlikely to make use of a bank or any other means of storing or transferring value, and although research carried out for one UK report (Matrix, 2007) suggests that such sums are readily attained even by high turnover 'drug mules', it is impossible properly to esti-

6 It is important to focus on *gross* revenues because estimating *net* revenues requires information about what DTOs pay to produce or purchase the drugs, and data are far too poor to permit this properly.

mate what share of these revenues will require laundering. (Though using largely hypothetical assumptions and extravagant extrapolations, anyone can guess at laundering figures, and unsurprisingly, some have done so: see Walker and Unger, 2009).

IV. Discussion and conclusions

A substantive review of organised crime and corruption policy would require more space and time than are available here. All that is possible is to point us in the direction of some key questions that are either unanswered or only very partially answered in the evidence available today. Most notably for this chapter (although each of the other factors play a role in this), it is useful to think about the processes that corrupting the enforcement process may involve. Applying these modes and patterns of thinking to the contemporary example of transnational bribery in relation to organised crime, or the organisation of serious crimes, is useful here. The concepts of corruption and bribery are often used synonymously. International conventions, principally the UNCAC and the OECD Anti-Bribery Convention, focus explicitly on bribery as the main tool of corruption that requires controlling. As the literature indicates, long term transnational organised crime requires corruption, and corruption requires a certain degree of organisation, but to what extent are those involved with transnational bribery also involved in (conventionally defined) organised crimes? Transnational bribery of foreign public officials often involves corporations looking to win or maintain public contracts. Such bribery may involve numerous agents, intermediaries, shell firms and clients in relation to the offering, giving, receiving and/or soliciting of bribes or other inducements in return for acts, services or omissions. There are many complexities in this area and the processes and actors involved are therefore many. Is it possible to demarcate and delineate the complex relations that exist between corruption of this type and organised crime? To do so, the concrete phenomena and processes that researchers addressing the gaps in the corruption and organised crime literature may want to explain and understand could include the following:

- How is bribe paying organised and financed, and what are the 'business' processes involved? E.g., how are finances for bribes such as slush funds created and which processes allow money to be transferred and paid? In cash, electronically or via other mechanisms such as transfers of businesses, corporately held real estate, etcetera?
- How are bribe givers and bribe receivers recruited? E.g., how are individuals within corporations and/or agents and intermediaries overseas recruited to pay bribes? Which criteria identify potential bribe receivers, agents and/or law enforcement officials?
- Which skills and abilities characterise the criminal types needed to carry out organised corrupt activities? E.g., financial and technological competence, persuasive personalities.
- Can a typology be created incorporating the level of bribe (small one-off payments to traffic or border police; 'acquiring' government officials on a longer-term basis; systematic bribing of politicians, etc), criminal type (level of crime specialisation etc), and the links between organised crime group and corrupt activities (business-organised crime group relations etc)?
- To what extent are the bribe givers or bribe receivers involved in other crime groups or criminal activities? E.g. do intermediaries provide other services or carry out other crimes such as frauds or racketeering? Are corrupt law enforcement officers also actively involved in enterprise crime?
- How do legal frameworks and/or enforcement activities addressing corruption or organised crime at the (inter)national level overlap, impact on each other, and shape the bribe paying landscape? E.g., civil recovery mechanisms for unspecified proceeds of crime; unexplained wealth laws plus official wealth declarations of a kind more common in Latin America than in the EU, where it is legally problematic and regarded as culturally inappropriate to put in place transparency mechanisms such as declarations of assets.

- How do public, private, third sector and inter-governmental bodies shape the control and policing of corruption and organised crime and how does this hinder corrupt regimes and/or individuals? E.g. self-regulation and moral entrepreneurs (see Lord, in preparation). What is the role of Financial Intelligence Units and general anti-money laundering regulations in both developed and developing countries bringing such intelligence to light (Levi, 2009)?
- What is the relationship between organised crime, corruption and the criminalisation of strongly desired activities, whether they be the consumption of drugs, of untaxed alcohol and tobacco products, or crossing national borders?

Once the above questions are empirically understood, the links between organised crime and corruption begin to emerge. It is obvious that drugs criminalisation stimulates corruption in producer, transit and consumer countries, and also that such criminalisation has not led to low consumption of illegal drugs in the West (which is not to state that it has had no use-reducing effects). The rise in drugs trafficking from Colombia via what are often termed 'weak states' in West Africa is merely one example of corruption-fuelled diversification to avoid controls that have *some* preventative effect on supplies. Their impact in West Africa depends on how widely the corrupt payments are shared, and on leakage of drug use there. However, the rewards of drug entrepreneurship tend to exceed those of legitimate entrepreneurship. Part of the toxic legacy of heroin and heroin policy is its impact on grand and petit corruption in Afghanistan and Pakistan. Yet the reference to untaxed booze and tobacco and to illegal migration indicate the complexity of this issue, whatever one's views about drugs policies. Do we lower taxes (and the health benefits from reduced toxicity) because of corruption risks? Do we have unrestricted immigration to reduce corruption risks? Corruption risks are part of the policy mix, but they are not a trump card in the debate. The reduction of corruption in law enforcement and transportation is a cross-border as well as an internal matter, and anti-corruption powers, resources (including financial investigation) and political will are important.

Another key area where there is a significant degree of overlap is related to the law and the enforcement agencies that investigate and prosecute these activities. If we consider the UK here – an unlikely place for an alliance between elites and 'organised crime' as conventionally understood – in transnational bribery, for example, any financial benefits created as a result of paying bribes may be considered proceeds of crime for the purposes of the Proceeds of Crime Act 2002 (POCA). Such proceeds may be confiscated in the UK through civil confiscation orders and civil recovery orders. This is also the case in other jurisdictions such as Germany, where prosecutors, although limited in civil law to fine corporations a maximum of EUR 1m, are additionally able to confiscate any profit made from the paying of the bribe.

Once the UK Bribery Act 2010 comes into force, individuals and corporations will be required to inform the Serious Organised Crime Agency (SOCA) or its planned successor body, the National Crime Agency, of any facilitation payments made (see Raphael, 2010). Facilitation payments are prohibited under UK law. As we write, however, small one-off facilitation payments are unlikely to be prosecuted by the UK authorities (Guidance Notes, 2011), first because of limitations with regards the resources of SOCA and the SFO to fully enforce the law, and second, because discretion as well as a willingness to increase the reporting of criminal activity is likely to result in no prosecution or investigation. The real risk for business individuals making small facilitation payments (as well as the directors of companies who may become liable for aiding and abetting the payments) arises when the acquisition, use or possession of the criminal property (e.g. financial profit from such a payment) is not disclosed to the authorities. It is then that such individuals will be committing money laundering offences under POCA. Failure to report places the individual that makes the facilitation payment at risk of criminal prosecution for the offence of money laundering with potential for 14 years imprisonment and an unlimited fine.

Money laundering controls have come to be seen as an important tool for dealing with corruption, particularly in developing countries (Levi et al., 2007), and the recovery of illicitly acquired assets is one of the centrepieces of the UN Convention against Corruption 2005. The Iraq Oil for Food Program (IIC, 2005) was merely one example of the circumvention of sanctions, but this was never defined as an 'organised crime' issue, perhaps indicating the need to rethink our constructs of organised crime away from an implicit focus on the underworld and towards a more subtle view of the linkages between underworld and upperworld. (See Wrong, 2005, 2009 for some powerful insight into this interpenetration in the DRC and Kenya.) The range of activities and the ways in which wealth transfers are effected illustrate some of the difficulties in relating using AML measures to punish corruption. While grand corruption is identified with notorious dictators and their cronies, many other forms of corruption might be misunderstood if described as petty for they are not insubstantial. Large bribes are paid to border or internal law enforcement officials, to judicial officers or to those who control them not to proceed against criminals or their goods: the latter can be illegal (like narcotics), counterfeit (software and other intellectual property, alcohol, medicines, cigarettes, tobacco), or legal but untaxed smuggled dutiable genuine goods. Corruption can arise in any area of procurement. It can arise from the need to obtain licenses or from any other economic activity, depending on the corrupt person(s) span of control. Whatever the formal structures that exist in the country, 'economic intelligence' may be transmitted to the corrupt elite and may lead to demands for payment in order to avoid 'disruption'. But no formal bribes in the form of direct transfer of cash or bank transfer need take place, making the identification of the offence, proof of corruption (and laundering) and appropriate sanctions nearly impossible. Sometimes it is simply understood that if people want to do business in particular town or country, they have to buy or sell via businesses or professionals whom they know to be connected to elites, criminals or both.

We end with two outlines that we consider useful to help us think more clearly about strategies to combat organised crime and corruption, acknowledging that our understanding of the impacts of such measures on outcomes are very poorly understood. This, we hope, will be at least partly redressed in the future, though they remain both conceptually and empirically difficult tasks. We should appreciate that broader impacts on system legitimacy and a sense of justice may be worth pursuing for their own sake, even if they have only a modest demonstrable impact on other outcomes.

Box 3 A Model of Organised Crime Prevention (Adapted from Levi and Maguire, 2004)

Community approaches	1. Community crime prevention 2. Passive citizen participation: giving information about harms and risks, hotlines 3. Active citizen participation: civic action groups
Regulatory, disruption and non-justice system approaches	4. Regulatory policies, programmes and agencies (domestic and foreign, including NGOs, anti-corruption and international bodies such as the IMF and World Bank as well as OECD/FATF) 5. Routine and suspicious activity reporting by financial institutions and other bodies of funds transfers 6. Tax policy and programmes 7. Civil injunctions and other sanctions, including the racketeering laws and civil forfeiture 8. Military interventions 9. Security and secret intelligence services 10. Foreign policy and aid programmes (e.g. US 'certification' of countries as adequate/ inadequate in their anti-drugs measures)
Private sector involvement	11. Individual companies 12. Professional and industry associations 13. Special private sector committees 14. Anti-fraud and money laundering software 15. Private policing and forensic accounting

Box 4 A deterrence framework for action against corruption and organised crime

- Expected risk of discovery
  - From private and public policing
- Expected consequences of discovery
  - Harm to self-image/social stigma
  - Reduced future business opportunities
  - Financial penalties
  - Proceeds of crime/substitute asset forfeiture
  - Traditional criminal sanctions
  - *All dependent on whether they are expected to be discovered; how far information is expected to be spread; and whether the business is expected to be able to survive without crime*
- Actual consequences of discovery
  - Future economic/crime opportunities
  - Punishment (penal and social) and its effects on those convicted & on others

References

Albanese, J. S. (1995) 'Where Organized and White Collar Crime Meet: Predicting the Infiltration of Legitimate Business' in J. Albanese (ed.) *Contemporary Issues in Organised Crime*, Monsey, NY: Willow Tree Press.

Beare, M. E. (1997) 'Corruption and organized crime: Lessons from history' *Crime, Law and Social Change*, 28: 155–172.

Buscaglia, E. and van Dijk, J. (2003) 'Controlling organized crime and corruption in the public sector' *Forum on Crime and Society*, 3(1/2): 12–34.

Center for the Study of Democracy (CSD) (2007) *Organized Crime in Bulgaria: Markets and Trends*, Sofia: CSD. Available at: http://www.csd.bg/fileSrc.php?id=2394 <Accessed 11/02/2011>.

Center for the Study of Democracy (CSD) (2010) *Examining the Links between Organised Crime and Corruption*, Sofia: CSD. Available at: http://www.csd.bg/fileSrc.php?id=20216 <Accessed 11/02/2011>.

Davis, I., Hirst, C. and Mariani, B. (2001) *Organised crime, corruption and illicit arms trafficking in an enlarged EU*, London: Saferworld. Available at: http://www.saferworld.org.uk/downloads/pubdocs/Organised%20crime.pdf <Accessed 11/02/2011>.

della Porta, D. and Vannucci, A. (1999) *Corrupt Exchanges: Actors, Resources, and Mechanisms of Political Corruption*, New York: Aldine De Gruyter.

Edelhertz, H. and Overcast, T. D. (1993) *The Business of Organised Crime: An Assessment of Organised Crime Business-Type Activities and Their Implications for Law Enforcement*, California: Palmer Press.

Edwards, A. and Levi, M. (2008) 'Researching the organization of serious crimes' *Criminology and Criminal Justice*, 8(4): 363–388.

Edwards, R. (2008) 'Special Met unit to root out corrupt prison officers' *Daily Telegraph*. Available at: http://www.telegraph.co.uk/news/uknews/2033424/Special-Met-unit-to-root-out-corrupt-prison-officers.html <Accessed 11/02/2011>.

Ernst and Young (2010) *Global Fraud Survey*. Available at: http://www.ey.com/Publication/vwLUAssets/Driving_ethical_growth_-_new_markets,_new_challenges:_11th_Global_Fraud_Survey/$FILE/EY_11th_Global_Fraud_Survey.pdf <Accessed 11/02/2011>.

Eurobarometer (2006)*Opinions on organised, cross-border crime and corruption*, Special Eurobarometer 245. Available at: http://ec.europa.eu/public_opinion/archives/ebs/ebs_245_en.pdf <Accessed 11/02/2011>.

Europol (2009) *OCTA 2009 EU Organised Crime Threat Assessment*, The Hague, Netherlands. Available at: http://www.europol.europa.eu/publications/European_Organised_Crime_Threat_Assessment_%28OCTA%29/OCTA2009.pdf <Accessed 11/02/2011>.

Fickenauer, J. O. (2005) 'Problems of definition: what is organized crime?' *Trends in Organized Crime*, 8(3): 63–83.

Godson, R. (ed.) (2003) *Menace to Society. Political-Criminal Collaboration Around the World*, New Piscataway, NJ: Transaction Publishers.

Guidance Notes (2011) *The Bribery Act 2010: Guidance*, London: Ministry of Justice http://www.justice.gov.uk/guidance/docs/bribery-act-2010-guidance.pdf.

Hagan, F. (2006) ''Organized Crime' and 'organized crime': Indeterminate problems of definition' *Trends in Organized Crime*, 9(4): 127–137.

IIC (2005) *Manipulation of the Oil-for-Food Programme by the Iraqi Regime*, http://www.iic-offp.org/documents/IIC%20Final%20Report%2027Oct2005.pdf <Accessed 01/01/2011>.

Jacobs, J. B. and Peters, E. (2003) 'Labor Racketeering: The Mafia and the Unions' *Crime and Justice*, 30: 229–282.

Kilmer, B., Caulkins, J., Bond, B. and Reuter, P. (2010) *Reducing Drug Trafficking Revenues and Violence in Mexico: Would Legalizing Marijuana in California Help*? Santa Monica: Rand.

Korsell, L. and Skinnari, J. (2010) 'Situational prevention against unlawful influence from organized crime', in K. Bullock, R. Clarke and N. Tilley (eds.) *Situational Prevention of Organised Crimes*, Cullompton: Willan.

Kroll (2010/2011) *Global Fraud Report*. Available at: http://www.kroll.com/library/fraud/FraudReport_English-US_Oct10.pdf <Accessed 01/01/2011>.

Kugler, M., Verdier, T. and Zenou, Y. (2005) 'Organized crime, corruption and punishment' *Journal of Public Economics*, 89: 1639–1663.

Levi, M. (2007) 'The Organization of Serious Crimes' in M. Maguire, R. Morgan, R. Reiner (eds.) *The Oxford Handbook of Criminology*, 4th Ed., Oxford: Oxford University Press.

Levi, M. (2009) 'The Impact of Anti-Money Laundering Measures within Developing Countries against Proceeds of Corruption', Paper for Illicit Financial Flows Colloquium, Washington DC: World Bank.

Levi, M. and Maguire, M. (2004) 'Reducing and preventing organised crime: An evidence-based critique', *Crime, Law and Social Change*, 41 (5): 397–469.

Levi, M., Dakolias, M. and Greenberg, T. (2007) 'Money laundering and corruption', in *The Many Faces of Corruption: Tracking vulnerabilities at the sector level,* [Editors J. Edgardo Campos and S. Pradhan], Washington, DC: the World Bank.

Lord, N. (in preparation).

Maltz, M. (1994) 'Defining Organised Crime' in R. J. Kelly, K. L. Chin and R. Schatzberg (eds.) *Handbook of Organized Crime in the United States*, Westport, CT: Greenwood Press.

Matrix Research and Consultancy (2007) *The Illicit Drug Trade in the United Kingdom*, 2nd edition, London: Home Office. Online Report 20/07. http://www.homeoffice.gov.uk/rds/pdfs07/rdsolr2007.pdf < Accessed 01/01/2011>.

Miller, J. (2003) *Police Corruption in England and Wales: Assessment of Current Evidence*, Home Office Online Report 11/03. Available at: http://rds.homeoffice.gov.uk/rds/pdfs2/rdsolr1103.pdf <Accessed 11/02/2011>.

Naylor, R. (2003) 'Towards a general theory of profit-driven crimes', *British Journal of Criminology*, 43: 81–101.

Paoli, L. (2003) *Mafia Brotherhoods: Organized Crime, Italian Style*, Oxford: Oxford University Press.

PricewaterhouseCoopers (2007) *Global Economic Crime Survey.* Available at: http://www.pwc.com/en_GX/gx/economic-crime-survey/pdf/pwc_2007gecs.pdf <Accessed 11/02/2011>.

Raphael, M. (2010) *Blackstone's Guide to the Bribery Act 2010*, Oxford: Oxford University Press.

Reuter, Peter and Edwin M. Truman (2004) *Chasing Dirty Money* Washington, D.C., Institute for International Economics.

Ruggiero, V. (2010) 'Who corrupts whom? A criminal eco-system made in Italy' *Crime, Law and Social Change*, 54: 87–105.

Schneider, F. and Enste, D. (2000) 'Shadow Economies: Size, Causes, and Consequences.' *Journal of Economic Literature* 381:77–114.

Shen, A., Antonopoulos, G. A. and von Lampe, K. (2010) ''The Dragon Breathes Smoke': Cigarette Counterfeiting in the People's Republic of China' *British Journal of Criminology*, 50(2): 239–258.

van de Bunt, H. (2004) 'Police corruption in the Netherlands' in M. Amir and S. Einstein (eds.) *Police Corruption: Challenges for Developed Countries. Comparative Issues and Commissions of Inquiry*, London: The Office of International Criminal Justice.

van Dijk, J. (2007) 'Mafia markers: assessing organized crime and its impact upon societies' *Trends in Organized Crime*, 10: 39–56.

Van Duyne, P. (2010) 'Organised Crime (Threat) as a Policy Challenge: a Tautology', *VARSTVOSLOVJE, Journal of Criminal Justice and Security,* 12 (4): 355–366.

Walker, J. and Unger, B. (2009) 'Measuring Global Money Laundering: 'The Walker Gravity Model'', *Review of Law & Economics*: Vol. 5(2): 821–853.

Wrong, M. (2001) *In the Footsteps of Mr. Kurtz*, London: Fourth Estate.

Wrong, M. (2009) *It's Our Turn to Eat*, London: Fourth Estate.

EDWARD H. DAVIS

Transnational civil asset recovery of the proceeds of crime and corruption: a practical approach

I. Introduction

The misappropriation of assets through corruption is an unfortunate but inescapable reality that has plagued civilisation since organised government and money came together. Corruption in the modern age, and its impact on society, is perhaps worse than it has ever been, as gargantuan state budgets and infrastructure projects provide perhaps irresistible targets for corrupt actors. The conduct of corrupt actors is facilitated by technology-driven banking and financial systems that allow the proceeds of corruption to be literally sent around the world with the click of a computer mouse. As well, corrupt conduct is facilitated by a fraudster's ability to conceal their identity behind multi-layered corporate shields and secrecy havens with legal systems designed to allow bank accounts to be owned with relative anonymity.

Corruption is a truly global problem. In Russia, for instance, annual corruption is believed to be between USD 240 to USD 300 billion dollars.[1] In China, which has one of the largest economies in the world, corruption similarly is pegged in the hundreds of billions of dollars each year.[2] Corruption costs African countries collectively

1 Matt A. Vega, The Sarbanes-Oxley Act and the Culture of Bribery: Expanding the Scope of Private Whistleblower Suits to Overseas Employees, 46 Harv. J. on Legis. 425, 428 (2009).

2 Daniel Abebe & Jonathan S. Masur, International Agreements, Internal Heterogeneity, and Climate Change: The 'Two Chinas' Problem, 50 Va. J. Int'l L. 325, 337, 354 (2010).

more than USD 150 billion annually.[3] A study by the World Bank a few years ago estimated that corrupt governments, along with their business partners, take in excess of USD 1 trillion in bribes each year and more subtle forms of corruption impact another USD 1.5 trillion in procurement decisions.[4]

While the numbers certainly are not encouraging, this does not mean that victims[5] of corruption are helpless. In many cases, victims can recover a significant portion of their losses, either through actual recovery of the assets or money that were stolen by 'tracing' the proceeds to wherever the perpetrator has placed them, or by prosecuting claims against various actors in the liability chain. It may be impossible to completely prevent losses from corruption, but there are steps governments, government instrumentalities and others can follow to increase asset recoveries.

Also aiding victims in the recovery of their stolen patrimony is the fact that courts and legislatures around the world are becoming increasingly aware of the scope and nature of the problem and are responding in kind by providing remedies that assist the victims and their lawyers. This is evidenced by treaties, conventions, and national laws that seek to target corrupt actors and the ill-gotten gains they seek to hide. These laws and the remedies they provide are a work in progress and should be scrutinised by all stakeholders with the ultimate goal of fine-tuning and improving these tools against corruption.[6]

3 Presentation of Dr. Anwar Ibrahim, former Deputy Prime Minister of Malaysia, to the World Bank, June 19, 2006 (transcript by Federal News Service, Washington DC).

4 Thomas R. Snider & Won Kidane, Combating Corruption Through International Law in Africa: A Comparative Analysis, 40 Cornell Int'l L.J. 691, 692 n.4 (2007).

5 The author defines 'victims' in the context of corruption as the countries or government instrumentalities that are the targets of corruption (direct victims) and the taxpayers and citizens of those countries (indirect victims).

6 Many of these treaties and national laws seek to use the criminal justice system as either the sole or predominant mechanism to stop this flow of unlawfully obtained proceeds of corruption. The focus of many local laws and treaties, such as the OECD Anti-Bribery Convention and the FCPA and its foreign counterparts is to focus on punishing the bribe givers. I would submit that this approach is, at best, dealing with only half of the problem. We have to face the fact that even if we are able to take one company after another out of the 'bribe giving'

The need to educate appropriate stakeholders continues to be of paramount importance. Most in the anti-corruption community continue to refer to this topic – as do the treaties – as stolen 'asset' recovery. This label of 'asset' recovery is value laden and leads to stultified thinking when it comes to the recovery of stolen wealth. This topic should be defined as stolen 'value' or stolen 'wealth' recovery.

This is not an academic distinction. Many of the modern treaties and tomes on 'asset' recovery assume that there is a traceable asset waiting idly to be identified through tracing principles, then frozen and repatriated. That is usually the exception not the rule. Much of the 'value' to be gained – in the form of damages – can be found in claims against those who have layered and laundered the stolen wealth in such a way that tracing is either impossible or a very difficult and time consuming process. So one must not think of 'asset' recovery but must instead visualise the process as 'value' recovery.

Another area of on-going debate involves the process by which governmental victims of corruption respond to the problem. Historically, government victims of corruption turned to other governments to assist them in seeking the return of proceeds of corruption which are believed to be within the borders of the country from which help is requested. However, this approach has only met with extremely limited success and has done little to stem the flow of corruption.

This is because government-to-government co-operation can work well (but doesn't always) when an identified traceable fund or

business, there will likely be another to step into its place if the perceived rewards are high enough and the bribe takers are left untouched. In many countries the bribe takers operate with almost complete impunity. One of the premises of this paper is that the problem of corruption will remain rampant until there is an equal commitment to the punishment of the bribe takers. To be sure, that punishment has to come in part through criminal prosecution of the bribe takers and the bribe givers. However, the recent spate of large fines levied by the U.S. Department of Justice (US DOJ) and the US Securities and Exchange Commission (SEC) point to the limitations of this approach. In the last couple of years the US DOJ and SEC have levied and collected billions of dollars in fines and penalties against companies that have entered into deferred prosecution agreements or settlements on the heels of being charged with violating the FCPA. However, large-scale corruption goes largely unchecked. Moreover, the victim states received none of these fines and penalties.

asset purchased with corruption proceeds can be identified and found. It is generally accepted that in the entire modern period that 'asset recovery' has been 'on the radar screen' of state actors – roughly beginning with the attempts to recovery the national patrimony stolen by the Marcos regime in the Philippines 20 years ago – that only roughly USD 5 billion has been recovered in the entire world in that entire period.[7] When compared to the amount of national patrimony that is believed to have been secreted by corrupt actors in that same period (approximately USD 1 trillion per year worldwide for the past 20 years which would be on the conservative side) that means that less than 0.030% of stolen national patrimony has ever been recovered. Even if those numbers are off by a factor of 100% that would mean that less than 3% of stolen assets have ever been recovered from the corrupt actors who have stolen them. That is a woefully inadequate track record by any standard.

In fact, the potentially highest recoveries are in the nature of civil claims against corrupt actors, to wit: suing those who solicit the corruption or those who aid the corrupt actors and those who hide their assets for them – are not the type of claims that Governments can and do bring. That is because typically those types of inchoate claims for damages are not the types of claims that can or will be litigated by governments, no matter how well intentioned, as they are generally simply not configured to provide this type of assistance nor do they have the standing to do so.

The question then becomes: does the current dominant model for the recovery of corruption proceeds – largely relying on government to government criminal law based assistance – actually work? The short answer is that – supported by the lack of results – is that it does not work. It certainly does not work nearly well enough for it to be the dominant model. To date no single model of asset recovery has emerged that can fairly be said to be the winning formula for breaking the back of corruption.

7 Jean-Pierre Brun, Larissa Gray, Clive Scott & Kevin M. Stephenson, Asset Recovery Handbook, A Guide for Practitioners, available at http://www1.worldbank.org/publicsector/star_site/documents/arhandbook/ar_handbook_final.pdf

While that might seem like bad news – it is not. It means that we are in the midst of a grand worldwide experiment to develop a better model that produces results. Likely, no single approach will ever work. The world is a complex and diverse place and to think that one model, one way or one method will work consistently across diverse social, legal, and cultural boundaries would be naïve at best.

However, there is a new trend emerging. The emerging trend is using civil asset recovery teams and civil litigation devices alongside criminal options to maximise a corruption victim's recovery. When civil litigation is used in combination with aid from friendly governmental authorities, government victims can begin to hit the corrupt actors where they can be hurt – in their pocketbooks. Government victims increasingly prefer the use of this type of 'combined arms' method to locate and recover misappropriated assets or other value to compensate them for their losses. This paper will examine the uses of these civil litigation teams and certain of these civil litigation devices, including prejudgment remedies and discovery devices, as well as some types of substantive claims that, if successfully prosecuted, often lead to the recovery of value.[8]

8 The author, Edward H. Davis, Jr., a founding shareholder of the international litigation and arbitration law firm Astigarraga Davis in Miami, primarily represents banking, corporate and governmental victims of serious fraud and grand corruption in the investigation and prosecution of civil fraud matters. His practice includes locating, freezing and recovering missing assets in the US and in numerous jurisdictions including Latin America, the Caribbean and Europe with a special focus on so-called secrecy havens. He also co-ordinates related multi-jurisdictional litigation and serves as a liaison with criminal authorities on behalf of his client-victims. Davis also represents creditors and various financial institutions in operational banking, creditor's rights and bankruptcy actions, including execution proceedings, fraudulent transfer cases and the domestication of foreign judgments. The author practices in the state of Florida, and thus ordinarily relies primarily on Florida-based principles and rulings of law. Thus, while it is of course impossible to discuss every country's civil litigation remedies relating to misappropriated assets, the author has done his best to discuss remedies that collectively should give a representative 'snapshot' of the most common types of asset recovery remedies under the law of the U.S. and other countries. Having said that, the remedies discussed in this article by no means represent an exhaustive list of the ones available either in the US or elsewhere.

II. The civil action recovery teams

The successful recovery of value misappropriated by corruption and other forms of financial fraud usually is a challenging task. It can, however, be made more feasible by the utilisation of the right resources. In particular, because thefts today are likely to be multi-jurisdictional and complex, having a sophisticated, experienced, team of professionals often will increase the chances of recovery.[9] Criminals exploit gaps; to wit: gaps in knowledge, timing, enforcement, informational flow and resources. These gaps can be eliminated in some cases or severely limited in others by employing the right team to recover the stolen value.

Recovery through private civil actions works through the use of Civil Action Recovery Teams or 'CARTs.' These are multi-disciplinary teams of professionals that work closely with the victimised state or state agency to plan and carry out a strategy to trace, trap and repatriate stolen wealth. They are not usually large teams and they are comprised of uniquely qualified professionals that are experienced in the recovery of stolen wealth such as members of the ICC's Fraud-Net and/or the AREN of the ICAR.

The premise is that the use of a CART under the direction of the victim government or government agency will act as an important component to deter public corruption by effectively increasing the recoveries of stolen assets. Countering corrupt actors and their accomplices to trace, recover and ultimately repatriate hidden stolen wealth requires expertise, specialised knowledge, disciplined co-ordination and legal agility. These capabilities and resources can also be brought to bear in designing and implementing a stolen wealth recovery framework that can take the gain out of the criminal enterprises operated by criminals with impunity. That is where the proposed team of

9 Indeed, the corrupt actors almost always have better resources than the victims who are pursuing them. Many times they have stolen tens of millions – if not hundreds of millions – of dollars and they have a powerful incentive to protect the lucre of their crimes.

specialised private sector professionals can provide value to the victimized State.

Because each case is unique, there is no 'one size fits all approach' – rather, each case must be evaluated and a determination must be made as to how best the assets and value might be recovered. Generally speaking, though, most CARTs will involve a team leader (usually a lawyer), legal counsel, forensic accountants and investigators.

Team leader

While most fraud recovery efforts will involve not one but rather several individuals, in the typical case it is imperative that there be a team 'leader.' This will usually, but not always, be legal counsel. Sometimes this can be in the form of an experienced insolvency practitioner if insolvency is involved. This person will spearhead the effort among the members of the team and will devise and implement the overall strategy behind the recovery effort. The team leader will be responsible for numerous aspects of the asset recovery effort. One is to define the overall objectives of the asset recovery effort which will be done by working closely with the client government and other members of the team. In most cases, of course, the objective will be to recover as much of the misappropriated proceeds of the fraud or corruption as possible and then seek to fill the gap by pursuing damage claims.

There are multiple issues to consider as to where to focus one's efforts. Many times the focus will be on the most accessible of the assets to help finance the rest of the recovery effort. In other cases, there is a logical order of pursuing assets depending upon the sequencing of the availability of proof available at the time. As one asset is pursued and recovered, the effort involved will likely provide new evidence to pursue the next asset. Further, if assets have been distributed in different countries, it may be more efficient to focus the recovery efforts on just one or a few of those countries, rather than all of them at the same time. This and other choices must be decided by the client, with the advice of the team leader. In other words, the client and the team leader must define 'win' at the outset of the case (which can and usually is refined as the case proceeds along), meaning the client must decide what it hopes to accomplish as a result of the recovery efforts. Many times there are multiple potential goals, some of which can even be mutually exclusive, requiring hard choices to be made at the outset or along the way.

The team leader also will do what it takes to be able to reach the assets wherever they may have been taken – in essence to equip the team to have a 'global reach.' This will entail locating and securing the legal, forensic and investigative resources in the places where the assets are believed to be located. For instance, if in a particular case, by way of example, it is thought that assets were secreted in Liechtenstein, it is critical to work with a Vaduz-based lawyer as early in the process as possible. The key here is to hire professionals who are experienced in asset recovery efforts. This is not an opportunity for the team leader to hire his law school classmates or to reciprocate for past referrals by engaging a lawyer that does not understand and does not have a proven track record in this complex area of the law. Along these lines, the team leader will be responsible for co-ordinating among the various jurisdictions involved, including taking on the role of instructing counsel. In doing all this, the team leader must be vigilant of preventing privileged and confidential information from being misused by any member of the team. And perhaps most important of all, in doing all this it will be necessary for the team leader to take all actions necessary to secure whatever evidence exists of the criminal's work, as well as to prevent additional assets from being misappropriated or further secreted after the theft is discovered. This could range from fairly straightforward steps, like alerting financial institutions to the theft, to more complex actions like petitioning tribunals for worldwide injunctive relief.

In short, while most value recovery efforts will involve many individuals, in most cases it is important that there be a team leader, usually legal counsel experienced in international asset recovery, to spearhead and devise the overall effort.[10]

10 For a list of such types of counsel visit the ICC – Fraudnet website at www.icc-fraudnet.com.

Legal counsel

The lawyer engaged by a victim might properly be seen as the central figure in the investigation and, ultimately in the prosecution of legal actions and the recovery of assets and value. Counsel will be responsible for initially analysing the scope of the corruption and then developing an overall strategy on how best to proceed. Among their responsibilities will be the hiring of appropriate individuals such as accountants, investigators and local counsel, to ensure that the team is working cohesively and that each team member has all of the available tools and information available to the lawyer. And as is often the case, when dealing with theft that is multi-jurisdictional, the lawyer will co-ordinate with all of the jurisdictions involved, usually with the help of local counsel, so that neither the criminal nor stolen assets will be left untouched simply because of their removal to another country. This may be done by utilising legal processes in those countries, such as injunctions or victim commenced criminal proceedings, as may be needed. The lawyer also will work to preserve as much evidence as possible and will be in the best position to preserve privileges and to understand the differences in legal cultures which must be harmonised when dealing with multi-jurisdictional asset recoveries. The key is to engage counsel who knows how to run or work within multi-capability teams and manage various simultaneous legal actions. The physical location of that counsel is much less important than the experience they bring to the table.

Forensic accountant

Forensic accounting can be thought of as the integration of accounting, auditing, and investigative skills, and as its name suggests, is a type of accounting analysis that is suitable for use in a courtroom or tribunal. A forensic accountant would be indispensable in most corruption cases, as it might be impossible to recover or trace stolen assets without an analysis of this type. And forensic accounting often proves invaluable in detecting fraud in the first place, through auditing. This is perhaps even truer when dealing with complex fraud and grand corruption, as the fraudster tends to be sophisticated and well financed and thus better equipped to hide the proceeds of the theft.

Typically, a forensic accountant will begin the investigating by examining financial records and meeting with individuals, to the extent possible, who would have the most knowledge about the theft or fraud (other than the perpetrator, of course). From that investigation, the forensic accountant will develop a report that will contain information relating to damages caused as a result of the theft or fraud, a summary of how the theft or fraud occurred and the transactions representing the theft or fraud, and hopefully, a tracing of the assets so that at least some of them can be recovered by the victim. Usually, a forensic accountant (not necessarily the same one used to perform the forensic examination) will testify in person at the trial or at interlocutory proceedings.

Investigator

Investigators also will play a crucial role in the recovery of assets. These resources will primarily be responsible for finding details about the theft or fraud – who was involved, where they are now, how it was done, where the assets were moved to, etc., with the ultimate goals being to recover as much of the stolen assets as possible, and possibly, to facilitate bringing the criminal to justice. The investigator must work closely with the forensic accountant and the lawyers involved in the case to ensure that each member of the team is up to date with respect to the information available. The most valuable information likely will come from witnesses on the inside of the theft or fraud. In most cases, along with a forensic accountant and other members of the team, the investigator will focus on gathering valuable documentary information to be used to support a circumstantial case.

III. Challenges to the use of civil action recovery teams

The biggest challenge to the use of a CART is the bias and misperception that the bringing of private civil actions by victimised States is not allowed or that there is some requirement that criminal or diplomatic channels be used exclusively or even primarily. Nothing could be further from the truth but many still cling to this cumbersome, slow and largely ineffective paradigm.

The next hurdle that must be overcome in the use of CARTs is obtaining proper funding for bringing the action or actions. Many times government coffers are already strained providing basic services to the citizenry and they have been further weakened by the very corruption that the civil action seeks to rectify. The easiest way to fund these cases is to realise that you usually don't have to fund the whole case at the outset. Usually there is some 'low hanging fruit' in the form of an asset or account that can be picked off at the very beginning of the case that can then be used to fund a good portion of the rest of the case.

Also, many lawyers and other professionals will undertake these cases, at least in part, on some form of a combined reduced hourly and contingency fee arrangement or with a conditional fee agreement that lowers the upfront outlay by rewarding the professionals at the conclusion if they recover the stolen value. This allows the victimised State to share the risk in a form of partnership with its CART to keep the pressure on the public treasury to a minimum. There are also some funds created by governments and NSAs to fund these types of cases that are beginning to emerge. Unfortunately, this avenue is developing slowly.

Lastly in this regard, there are now private funders in the form of venture capitalists and hedge funds that are creating lawsuit funding companies. These funding entities provide capital to finance the case in exchange for a cut of the recovered proceeds. There are obvious political implications to these arrangements but they are now a viable alternative.

Another challenge to the use of private civil actions by CARTs is the ability to allege and prove damages. What is the proper measure of damages in a corruption case? Is it the amount of the bribe? That seems like a slap on the wrist that many large corrupt bribe payers would be happy to pay as it will be a fraction of their profit. Is it the value of the gross profit made on the corrupt deal? Is it the value of the 'net profit' made on the corrupt deal? Isn't using net profit as a measure of damages akin to giving the bank robber a credit for the cost of the gun and bullets and the ski mask used in the robbery against what they must pay back? Why should a company get to net out its fixed costs or its overhead before paying back what is effectively stolen through corrupt conduct? Or is it some other measure? This area of the law is still being developed. The damage to a victimised State goes well beyond 'dollars and cents.' How does one value the cost to a society of the loss of trust and faith in its political system, the corrosive effect on its political system or the energy and cost that the government must expend to obtain the return of what was rightfully its to begin with? There is a movement afoot to establish a new definition of corruption damages referred to as 'Societal Damages.' This is a new concept and it cries out for study by the international anti-corruption community.

The last great challenge to this model is the cross-border collection of evidence. At one time this seemed like an almost insurmountable challenge. However, through the development of many procedural devices such as 28 U.S.C. § 1782 and Chapter 15 of the US Bankruptcy Code in the US, Anton Piller and Banker's Trust orders in the UK, '*prueba anticipada*' and '*acción exhibitoria*' procedures in Latin countries and the new Swiss civil procedure code which went into effect on January 1, 2011, the ability to civilly gather evidence internationally for use against corrupt actors has dramatically increased. Now a well-led and staffed CART can gather evidence simultaneously in multiple countries and use it to build a case to make a proprietary claim to stolen wealth. Oftentimes this evidence can be gathered with a 'gag and a seal' so that the corrupt actors never even know the CART is closing in on them.

IV. Prejudgment remedies

In addition to having a team of competent professionals, in many cases the use of prejudgment remedies can be a 'game-changer' in terms of the victim's ultimate success in recovering any misappropriated assets. That is because often it will be impossible or nearly impossible for the victim to even begin a lawsuit against the perpetrators without the sort of information that can be gained through the use of prejudgment remedies. Even where the victim knows where the assets have been misappropriated, prejudgment remedies like injunctions or freeze orders play a crucial role in that they make it harder for the perpetrators to move the assets to another place pending the resolution of the lawsuit.

The role of reciprocity

Before delving into specific prejudgment remedies, however, it is worth pausing to note the importance of judicial intervention in cases of fraud, corruption, and the like in multinational treaties, as mentioned earlier. Such cross-border co-operation regarding the recovery of misappropriated assets has gone a long way to helping victims. Indeed, more generally speaking, reciprocity is an important factor in the enforcement of prejudgment remedies. One reason for this is that the refusal by a foreign court to recognise or enforce a domestic prejudgment order, such as an injunction, could lead the domestic court to similarly refuse an order from the same foreign court. For instance, if a US-based victim were to petition a court in the Bahamas for an order permitting access to documents from a Bahamian bank and that petition were denied, the corresponding US court might refuse to honour an order from the Bahamian court.

Injunctions

Injunctions are good examples of this principle. While they can be immensely useful to preserve the *status quo* and prevent the perpetrator from moving the assets to another location, some countries' courts are reticent to enforce an injunction issued by another country, at least if the injunction is a preliminary and not a permanent injunction. In the case of Pilkington Bros. v. AFG Industries,[11] the District Court denied enforcement of an interim injunction against the disclosure of trade secrets entered by a British court. While the Pilkington court did not go so far as issuing a bright-line ruling against enforcement of all foreign interim injunctions, and instead held that the question was one to be decided on a case-by-case basis, the court expressed concern that enforcing the injunction would interfere with the proceedings underway in England. For instance, if the enjoined party were alleged to have breached the injunction, it would be required to interpret the injunction and this could result in a different interpretation than that of the issuing court.

One potential way to circumvent the result reached in Pilkington is to have the foreign court issue some sort of judgment instead of an interim injunction, and then petition the domestic court for an injunction to enforce the judgment. The court in Clarkson Co. v. Shaheen[12] issued a preliminary injunction requiring records to be turned over and restraining the alienation of any corporate property, based on the entry of a bankruptcy judgment in a Canadian court.

Florida courts have squarely addressed the enforceability of foreign injunctions. In 1995, the Third District Court of Appeals of Florida, in Nahar v. Nahar[13] receded from a prior opinion in Cardenas v. Solis, which had limited enforcement of foreign preliminary injunctions to very specific circumstances.[14] The Cardenas court had held that:

[A]s a general rule, only the final judgments of courts of a foreign country are subject to enforcement and recognition in this country,

11 581 F. Supp. 1039 (D. Del. 1984).

12 544 F.2d 624 (2d Cir. 1976).

13 656 So. 2d 225, 229 (Fla. 3d DCA 1995).

14 570 So. 2d 996 (Fla. 3d DCA 1990).

provided certain jurisdictional and due process standards are observed by the foreign court; non-final and interlocutory orders of foreign courts, however, are not entitled to such recognition or enforcement.[15]

Notwithstanding, the Cardenas court enforced a Guatemalan temporary injunction in a domestic relations case, explaining that foreign interlocutory orders were enforceable in two contexts: (1) creditors rights and (2) spousal and childrens' rights in domestic relations cases.

In Nahar, the Court held that the better approach was to follow the Restatement (Second) Conflict of Laws §§ 92 and 98 in their entirety. The Nahar court dispensed with general rules requiring determination of finality and subject matter, declaring that

> Any foreign decree should be recognized as a valid judgment and thus be entitled to comity where the parties have been given notice and the opportunity to be heard, where the foreign court had original jurisdiction, and where the foreign decree does not offend the public policy of the State of Florida.[16]

The Court went on to hold that '[w]here a party has had notice and opportunity to be heard and the foreign court has satisfied Florida's jurisdictional and due process requirements their orders will be entitled to comity.'[17]

Prejudgment seizures and other prejudgment remedies

The availability of prejudgment remedies naturally will, of course, depend on which country's laws are at issue. For instance, generally speaking, in the US, prejudgment seizures are hard to obtain, partially because courts have struck down statutes (including one from Florida in the case of Fuentes v. Shevin, 407 U.S. 67 (1972)) that they perceived to be too aggressive or violative of a party's constitutional rights. To the extent prejudgment seizures exist in the U.S., they must afford the affected party due process rights, namely notice and opportunity to be heard, and often a monetary bond to compensate the af-

15 Id. at 998 (Fla. 3d DCA 1990).

16 Nahar, at 229 (Emphasis added).

17 Id. at 230.

fected party in the event the seizure later is found to be unlawful. Exceptions to this general rule include when: 1) the seizure is directly necessary to secure an important governmental or general public interest; 2) there is a need for very prompt action, or 3) when a state or government official is directly involved in the decision to seize the property, which affords at least minimum concern for the rights of the individual or entity being seized. See, e.g., Solomos v. Jenne, 776 So.2d 953 (Fla. 4th DCA 2000). And, at least in federal courts, prejudgment seizures cannot be used as a convenient means to secure payment for a future money judgment, for the Supreme Court in Grupo Mexicano De Desarrollo v. Alliance Bond Fund, 527 U.S. 308 (1999), held that federal courts do not have the power, 'equitable' or otherwise, to do so.

On the other hand, many civil law countries have a long-standing tradition of granting prejudgment remedies and injunctions. For instance, France has its 'Saisie Conservatoire,'[18] Italy its 'Sequestro,'[19] Germany its 'Arrest,'[20] and Spain and other countries the 'Embargo Preventivo.'[21] Such remedies are not limited to civil law countries, however.

Mareva injunctions

Since the decision of Mareva Compania Naviera S.A. v. International Bulk Carriers S.A. in 1975,[22] English courts have entered what is commonly called the 'Mareva Injunction.' The Mareva Injunction, codified in 1981 by incorporation into the Supreme Court Act, is an 'injunction restraining a party to any proceedings from removing from the jurisdiction of the high court or otherwise dealing with assets.'[23] In

18 Code de Procé Dure Civile [C. Pr. Civ.] Arts. 48–58, 557 to 582 (Fr.).

19 The Italian Civil Code, Release 93-1, translated by Mario Beltramo, Giovanni E. Longo, John H. Merryman, Dobbs Ferry, N.Y.: Oceana, §§ 1798–1802, 2768–2769, 2793, 2905–2906.

20 Zivilprozessordnung [ZPO] §§ 916–945 (W. Ger.).

21 Milliken & Farwell v. Sweet Home Co., 49 So. 669, 671 (La. 1909) (noting the Spanish civil code).

22 [1975] 2 Lloyds Rep. 509 (C.A.).

23 Supreme Court Act, Section 37(3).

1982, England became a party to the Brussels Convention.[24] The Convention, which provides for general rules of venue, jurisdiction and enforcement of awards and judgments between the signatory European countries, made the provisional measures available in any one contracting state available to litigants in all other contracting states.[25] Hence, under the Convention, all of its members may seek a Mareva Injunction.[26]

An example of a Mareva Injunction in effect is seen in a 1989 decision by the English Court of Appeal, which granted a 'worldwide' Mareva Injunction[27] against Haiti's former president, Jean Claude Duvalier, and some of his relatives at the request of the Haitian government.[28] The court issued an injunction over assets illegally acquired and removed from Haiti, *wherever* located. Although the Haitian litigation was pending in a French court, and most of the assets were not likely to be located in the United Kingdom, the Haitian government sought relief in England in order to obtain a Mareva Injunction that would enjoin Duvalier from disposing of any assets he may hold anywhere in the world. England presumably was chosen because it was the most likely jurisdiction to issue an order purporting to freeze the assets of Duvalier throughout the European Union. Mareva Injunctions are now known in the UK as 'Freezing Orders' while they are still known as Mareva Injunctions in some English commonwealth jurisdictions.

Prejudgment attachments

Regarding prejudgment attachment, under Florida law, a creditor may obtain a writ of attachment when a debtor is contractually indebted to

24 www.curia.eu.int/common/recdoc/convention/en/c-textes/_brux-textes.htm.

25 Civil Jurisdiction and Judgments Act, 1982, Ch. 27, § 25.

26 The development of the law of Mareva Injunctions is dynamic and beyond the scope of this paper, thus appropriate counsel should be sought from a qualified British Commonwealth counsel in this regard.

27 The English court called this injunction 'worldwide,' although it more likely only applied to contracting parties of the Brussels convention.

28 Republic of Haiti v. Duvalier, [1989] 2 W.L.R. 261 (C.A.).

him and the creditor can show the existence of one or more of the specific conditions set out in section 76.04 of the Florida Statutes. Section 76.04 provides that a creditor may acquire an attachment on a debt actually due to him when the debtor does one or more of the following:

1. Will fraudulently part with his property before judgment can be obtained against him;
2. Is actually removing his property out of state;
3. Is about to remove his property out of state;
4. Resides out of the state;
5. Is actually moving himself out of state;
6. Is about to move himself out of state;
7. Is absconding;
8. Is concealing himself;
9. Is secreting his property;
10. Is fraudulently disposing of his property;
11. Is actually removing himself beyond the limits of the judicial circuit in which he resides;
12. Is about to remove himself out of the limits of such judicial circuit.

Upon motion by the plaintiff, a writ of attachment may issue when the grounds relied on for the issuance of the writ *(i.e.,* the grounds specified in section 76.04)*, clearly appear from the specific facts shown by a verified complaint or a separate affidavit of the plaintiff.* Fla. Stat §76.08. The plaintiff may proceed with this motion on an *ex parte* basis, that is, without notice to the other side, where there is reason to believe that the property may be concealed or removed before the writ of attachment can be procured. Hordis Bros. v. Sentinel Holdings, Inc., 562 So. 2d 715, 718 (Fla. 3d DCA 1990).

A writ will be issued only when the plaintiff, his agent, or attorney posts a bond in at least double the debt demanded, and it must be sufficient to pay all costs and damages that the defendant sustains in the event the attachment is deemed to have been improvidently procured. Fla. Stat. § 76.12 (emphasis added).

Section 76.18 provides that after the execution of the writ, the property attached may be restored if the defendant posts a bond that exceeds the value of the property or claim by one fourth. Pursuant to section 76.24, the defendant also may obtain the dissolution of the writ of attachment by motion *unless* the plaintiff proves (a) the grounds upon which the writ was issued, *and* (b) a reasonable probability that final judgment in the underlying action will be rendered in its favour. Thus, where there is no basis for the entry of a money judgment against the defendant, a writ of attachment must be dissolved. See Cuba Aeropostal Agency, Inc. v. Kane, 145 So. 2d 764 (Fla. 3d DCA 1962). While this discussion of the remedy of attachment is focused on Florida law many such other similar remedies exist in other legal systems.

Prejudgment garnishments

'A prejudgment writ of garnishment. . . is a civil remedy available to a party to secure the anticipated money judgment the party ultimately expects to recover.' Garel and Jacobs, P.A. v. Wick, 683 So. 2d 184, 186 (3d DCA, 1996). In Florida, an action for a prejudgment writ of garnishment is considered 'ancillary to the main action,' and 'should only be sought where the primary obligation is sought to be enforced.' Id. Under section 77.031(2) of the Florida Statutes, a prejudgment writ of garnishment may be obtained by the plaintiff or the plaintiff's attorney upon the filing of:

A verified motion or affidavit alleging by specific facts the nature of the cause of action; the amount of the debt and that the debt for which the plaintiff sues is just, due, and unpaid; that the garnishment is not sued out to injure either the defendant or the garnishee and that the plaintiff believes that the defendant will not have in his or her possession, after execution is issued, tangible or intangible property in this state and in the county in which the action is pending on which a levy can be made sufficient to satisfy the plaintiff's claim. The writ of garnishment shall set forth a notice to the defendant of the right to an immediate hearing for dissolution of such writ pursuant to s. 77.07.

Id. Section 77.031(3) imposes the additional requirement that a bond in at least double the amount of the debt demanded be posted, just as with attachments, in order to cover costs and damages incurred by the garnishee in the event the garnishment later is deemed wrongful.

Finally, Florida law provides that prejudgment writs of garnishment may only be obtained with respect to certain causes of action. For instance, prejudgment garnishment may not be had for actions in tort. Fla. Stat. § 77.02. Once again, while this discussion is centred on Florida law other similar remedies exist in other jurisdictions around the world.

Declaratory relief

This is a way by which a litigant may obtain a court order 'declaring,' or clarifying, that it is owed something. As explained by one commentator:

> From the perspective of a party threatened with liability, declaratory judgment provides a means by which to avoid waiting until the opposing party finds it convenient to bring suit, possibly at a time after the damage has occurred . . . . Conversely, from the perspective of a potential plaintiff, declaratory judgment permits the settlement of controversies before the actions of the potential defendant develop into actual violations of law.[29]

Thus, a 'declaratory judgment provides [parties] with the benefit of an expedient and economical resolution to matters in dispute.' Id. While technically not a 'pre-judgment' remedy because the resolution of a petition for declaratory relief itself constitutes a judgment, this remedy nonetheless should be considered where appropriate because it may allow the victim of theft, fraud, etc. to establish his entitlement to the misappropriated assets faster than by a trial involving a more conventional basis for liability, such as a fraud claim.

In terms of federal law, the US Congress has enacted the Declaratory Judgment Act, which provides in part that

29 Lawrence M. Sung, Comment, Intellectual Property Protection or Protectionism? Declaratory Judgment Use by Patent Owners Against Prospective Infringers, 42 Am. U.L. Rev. 239 (1992).

> Any court of the United States, upon the filing of an appropriate pleading, may declare the rights and other legal relations of any interested party seeking such declaration, whether or not further relief is or could be sought. Any such declaration shall have the force and effect of a final judgment or decree and shall be reviewable as such.[30]

Florida and other states have enacted their own declaratory relief statutes, as well. E.g., Fla. Stat. § 86.011 et seq. Again, the concept of declaratory judgments is not uncommon through the world albeit with different elements and known by different names.

V. Tools in aid of actions to recover assets

Whether a lawsuit will succeed or fail often also will depend on what evidence the plaintiff can provide, of course, and this in turn many times will depend on what the plaintiff can find out, or 'discover.' This section will address some of the means available by which the plaintiff may accomplish this. The below is not meant to be an exhaustive list of discovery devices available, but rather to illustrate some of the more common or useful ones.

28 USC § 1782

This US federal statute allows the gathering of information and evidence to be used in proceedings in countries other than the US Section 1782 permits a federal district court, which acts as the trial court in the American federal legal system, to compel an individual within its jurisdiction to furnish evidence, whether by form of a statement or by producing documents, so that such evidence can be used in a foreign judicial proceeding. So, for example, the associate of a fraudster that was based in England but who absconded to the US since the commission of the fraud could be compelled to furnish testimony that could

30 28 U.S.C. § 2201(a) (2004).

then be used in any proceedings brought or reasonably contemplated in England against the fraudster. Section 1782 does have certain limitations. Probably the most significant one is that only the court located in the district in which the would-be witness is located has the power to compel the testimony or document production. This means that a district court in California, for instance, cannot order a witness in New York to testify or produce documents. This can be remedied by filing multiple 1782 actions where necessary.

Pure bills of discovery and like processes

This is a tool that allows a victim to file an action in court solely to obtain discovery, so that such discovery can then be used in an actual lawsuit later on. It can prove invaluable when a plaintiff has a good faith belief that it has a cause of action but lacks some of the information necessary to allege all the elements of the claim. In the case of fraud, this might come into play when the identity of a fraudster is known but the precise flow of funds is not yet known. In such a scenario, the fraud victim could file a pure bill of discovery in the appropriate court and ask the court to allow information to be obtained from financial institutions (with a gag and a seal where appropriate), through which hopefully the money flow can become known and then a substantive action could be filed against those involved and to freeze assets. In civil law countries there are similar devices (*e.g.*, *prueaba anticipada* or the *accion exhibitoria*) and in English jurisdictions there are the Banker's Trust and Anton Piller orders which can be powerful tools to obtain evidence in the recovery of assets.

Inchoate claims/choses in action

Inchoate claims are by definition claims that are not fully ripe, but will be ripen on the happening of a particular event. For instance, if the victim has evidence that a 'shill' bidder assisted the perpetrator in fraud in connection with a construction contract, but has not yet paid out the excess money under the contract, the claim arguably would be 'inchoate' until the money was paid out. Choses in action are somewhat related and involve a legal right to sue. While these are more in the nature of a 'claim' than discovery devices, under the right circumstances they can be used in the early stages of litigation to obtain discovery or pressure third parties that may have assisted or been involved with the misappropriation, such as banks, lawyers, accountants, etc.

Subpoenas and other discovery under Federal Rules of Civil Procedure

Most US states, such as Florida, still allow pure bills of discovery in the appropriate situations. In the American federal legal system, however, pure bills of discovery were expressly supplanted by the Federal Rules of Civil Procedure, which governs discovery among other things, and domestic discovery from non-parties to an action pursuant to those Rules is governed by Rule 45. Under Rule 45, an individual or company that is not a party to an action may nonetheless be compelled, by virtue of a subpoena, to provide testimony or documents. In order for Rule 45 to come into play, however, a substantive or plenary action must already be pending before the district court.

Besides Rule 45, there are other helpful provisions relating to discovery under the Federal Rules of Civil Procedure. For instance, Rule 28 allows depositions to be taken in a foreign country under a variety of circumstances, including pursuant to any applicable treaty or convention, a letter of request or letters rogatory, or notice if the witness is willing to appear voluntarily. The deposition then could be used in the action pending before the District Court.

Norwich Pharmacal/Bankers Trust Orders

These are used against financial institutions holding an account with money that belongs to the plaintiff, which money was obtained inequitably. Under the Norwich standard, a court can order a third party that was involved with the activities of the wrongdoer and accountholder to assist the victim by providing information, such as the identity of the wrongdoer. Per the Bankers Trust v. Shapira case,[31] the third party is to facilitate an asset trace.

Anton Piller (or private search and seizure) orders

These orders, which somewhat resemble discovery requests and subpoenas under seal in the American system, entitle a party to enter a premises – without notice – and search for pertinent items or documents. They are particularly useful where the victim is satisfied that the subject of the order will not disclose the fact of same to the perpetrator. And, since the search is done without notice, it minimizes the risk that records will be concealed or destroyed prior to the search. They have been used against lawyers, accountants and other service providers of perpetrators – basically, anyone who may possess information relevant to the perpetrator's assets and business.

Hague convention on the taking of evidence abroad in civil or commercial matters

The Hague Convention (codified in the U.S. at 28 USC § 1781) is another well-established means for taking evidence from an individual or company located abroad for use in local proceedings. Briefly, from the US perspective, the party seeking evidence pursuant to this manner would first petition the court in the US to issue a letter of request, often referred to as letters rogatory, in which the assistance of the court of the foreign country is requested. If the foreign country is a signatory to the Convention, service is accomplished usually by transmitting the letters rogatory to that country's designated 'Central Authority,' which is responsible for accepting service. The letters rogatory should either be written in the recipient country's language, or be accompanied by a certified translation into that language. The letters rogatory also must specify what evidence is sought. One should be aware that many countries have restrictions on the type of informa-

31 [1980] WLR 1274 (CA).

tion allowed to be obtained under the Hague Convention. For instance, France and Australia, among others, do not allow 'pre-trial' discovery, that is, discovery to be used before a lawsuit has been filed. And another drawback about discovery under the Convention is that often it is a slow and expensive process. Even with these and other limitations, however, the Convention can be a useful tool for obtaining discovery from foreign countries, and often is the only way to do so.

VI. Substantive claims or causes of action that may be used to recover assets

The preceding section focused on prejudgment remedies, i.e., remedies obtained before a final judgment in the underlying action is issued. This section addresses the substantive or actual claims or causes of action that are typically seen in lawsuits to recover misappropriated assets.

Overview and the importance of tracing

The successful recovery of misappropriated assets usually is a challenging task. From a legal perspective, one reason for this is that before a victim can utilize many of the tools or claims available to a victim, it will be necessary for the victim to be able to 'trace' his entitlement to the misappropriated assets, meaning he will have to show a link between point A and point B, A being where the assets were stolen from the victim (say, a bank account) and B being the present location or form of the stolen assets (an offshore haven, a fancy sports car, etc.). This requirement, while perhaps seeming harsh at first glance, is imposed primarily to prevent a victim from mistakenly or inadvertently affecting an innocent third-party's assets in the quest to recover the misappropriated assets from the true criminal. That is, requiring the victim to fulfil the tracing requirement makes it much more likely that only assets belonging to the victim will be affected.

Constructive trusts and equitable liens

It would not be practical to attempt to list every type of claim for the recovery of misappropriated assets even under American law, let alone under the laws of every country. One obvious reason for this is that the elements and proof needed for claims like fraud, breach of fiduciary duty, and the like will differ from jurisdiction to jurisdiction. This section narrows the focus to two types of substantive remedies, to wit: constructive trusts and equitable liens. These were chosen because both the U.S. and other countries that widely use these remedies find that they are predicate for recovery under many other types of claims. They also serve as useful examples of the importance of a plaintiff's ability to trace his misappropriated assets into the perpetrator's possession.

Constructive trust

Assuming the victim is able to track down the misappropriated assets, the legal remedy of constructive trust may prove to be useful. It is recognized not only in just about every American jurisdiction but also in other countries, such as England. As one famous jurist described it, constructive trust is 'the formula through which the conscience of equity finds expression. When property has been acquired in such circumstances that the holder of the legal title may not in good conscience retain the beneficial interest equity converts him into a trustee.'[32] In other words, it is a legal fiction by which the criminal is regarded as holding the stolen assets 'in trust' for the rightful owner. Thus, to the extent a victim is able to prove that it is the true owner of assets in the hands of the criminal (usually by the use of 'tracing' principles), it may be possible for the victim to impose a constructive trust over the assets so that they can be recouped. Of course, that a constructive trust may lie only over assets whose ownership can be traced to the victim means that a constructive trust may not be had

32 Benjamin Cardozo, Beatty v. Guggenheim Exploration Co., 122 N.E. 378, 380 (N.Y. Ct. Apps. 1919).

over a fraudster's general assets. By the same token, if the fraudster has used up or converted the original assets into something else, as, for example, when stolen cash is used to buy a product, or is joined with other assets not belonging to the victim, or is simply spent, constructive trust will not be available. Rather, in such circumstances, the victim likely would resort to the remedy of *equitable lien*.

Equitable lien

Equitable liens is a legal remedy that is similar to constructive trusts in that 'their basic purposes [are] to identify and impress upon certain property the beneficial rights that have arisen in an innocent party who in some way contributed to the acquisition, protection or improvement of that property.'[33] Like constructive trusts, it is recognized everywhere in the U.S. and in other countries. Where equitable liens and constructive trusts mainly differ is how they are used. Equitable liens are superior to constructive trusts in two broad situations: when misappropriated assets do not exist in the same form as when they were taken (for example, when cash is stolen and used to buy an automobile), or when the victim can show that the criminal has misappropriated its assets, but is unable to pinpoint the particular asset (again using the example of stolen cash, this would apply if the stolen cash were deposited into the fraudster's bank account and commingled with other funds). In such circumstances, a constructive trust could not be imposed because the misappropriated assets no longer exist or were combined with other assets, but an equitable lien would be available, and the lien would be imposed on the criminal's general assets up to the value of the misappropriated assets. In the example of the stolen cash being used in part to purchase a ranch, a lien could be imposed on the ranch equal to the amount of the stolen cash.

33 Holder v. Williams, 334 P.2d 291, 292 (Cal. App. 1959).

Chapter 15 of the United States Bankruptcy Code

A final example of a powerful asset recovery tool is Chapter 15 of the US Bankruptcy Code, which was added by Congress in 2005 as part of an extensive overhaul of the Code known as the Bankruptcy Abuse Prevention and Consumer Protection Act of 2005. Chapter 15 represents a potentially very powerful tool in the tracing and recovery of assets, with one important caveat – its applicability presupposes the existence of a pending insolvency, liquidation, bankruptcy, or like proceeding in a country other than the U.S.

Chapter 15 was based on the Model Law on Cross-Border Insolvency, which was developed by the UNCITRAL.[34] The main purpose of Chapter 15 is to promote co-operation between countries in international insolvency situations by giving recognition to foreign proceedings and allowing access to these proceedings by representatives of the foreign bankruptcy debtor. A brief overview of the procedure under Chapter 15 may be helpful. It is essentially a two-step process. Initially, a representative of the foreign estate files an application for recognition in a bankruptcy court in the US. Along with the petition, the representative files a certified copy of the foreign court papers commencing the foreign proceeding and naming the foreign representative, a certificate from the foreign court affirming that the proceeding and the representative are still in existence, and a statement identifying all other known foreign proceedings involving the debtor. Provided that the papers are in order, the petition will usually be granted.

Upon the granting of the petition, certain sections of the Bankruptcy Code come into effect automatically, the most notable of which probably is section 362, title 11, known as the 'automatic stay' provision. This provision is very powerful, as it prevents almost all types of legal actions against the estate and its assets from occurring, absent court permission. Additionally, the foreign representative is granted

34 This model law has also been adopted in the following countries: Australia, Canada, Colombia, Eritrea, Greece, Japan, Mauritius, Mexico, Montenegro, New Zealand, Poland, Republic of Korea, Romania, Serbia, Slovenia, South Africa, United Kingdom of Great Britain and Northern Ireland and the British Virgin Islands.

certain powers, such as the right to use, sell, or lease the estate's property pursuant to section 363, title 11.

But, perhaps the most important aspect of Chapter 15 as relates to fraud cases and the recovery of assets is the discovery powers that it gives to foreign representatives. Under section 1521(a)(4) of title 11, a foreign representative may obtain broad discovery, including 'the examination of witnesses, the taking of evidence or the delivery of information concerning the debtor's assets, affairs, rights, obligations, or liabilities.' Indeed, the scope of discovery that is available under section 1521(a)(4) is akin to the broad discovery provided for by Federal Rule of Bankruptcy Procedure 2004. While this has been likened by some courts as permitting a 'fishing expedition' to discover information concerning the estate's assets and liabilities,[35] the prudent practitioner will focus all requests to not draw such a challenge.

So how does this apply in the context of asset recovery? It was mentioned earlier that Chapter 15 applies only when there is a foreign insolvency, liquidation, bankruptcy or like proceeding pending. Practically speaking, then, Chapter 15 would apply in two broad categories of fraud cases: those in which a shell or artificial company was used as an instrument by the fraudster or those in which the fraud occurred in a legitimate company either of which can be wound up, liquidated or placed in receivership.

Neither scenario is hard to imagine, of course. As to the first, it is no secret that fraudsters often will use a shell company (usually more than one) as vehicles for their fraudulent schemes, for instance the creation of, a bank with no real customers to give the air of legitimacy to a swindle.[36] For the second, the typical scenario is a formerly good company 'gone bad' in which a 'midstream' fraud occurs either due to mismanagement, financial statement fraud or the intervention of wrongdoer who gets control of the company to use it for improper purposes.

For Chapter 15 to apply, then, there would need to be pending insolvency proceedings in a foreign country under either scenario. After

35 E.g., In re Duratech Industries, Inc., 241 B.R. 283 (E.D. N.Y. 1999).

36 The widespread use of shell companies in fraudulent and other illicit activities was noted in a 2006 report by the U.S.'s FinCen, available at http://www.fincen.gov/LLCAssessment_FINAL.pdf.

commencement of the foreign proceedings, the person appointed as representative in those proceedings could then file a petition for recognition under Chapter 15, as described above, and upon approval, could benefit from its provisions. In summary, while Chapter 15 does not apply in every fraud case, in the cases that it does apply, it can be a powerful tool against the fraudster.

VII. Conclusion

There is no doubt that corruption and other forms of financial fraud are a plague on modern society, particularly in developing countries. With today's borderless economy and ever-evolving technology, fraud and corruption are problems that are here to stay, and likely to continue to worsen. Fortunately, as courts and legislatures become aware of this ever-growing problem, victims have more and more legal devices and tools available to them. CARTs using remedies (including prejudgment remedies) that help prevent the perpetrator from further moving or dissipation of the assets and expanded options by which to obtain discovery, especially in the hands of a team of competent professionals, combined with aid from governmental authorities, are increasingly assisting victims to locate and recover misappropriated assets and successfully prosecute claims against those who assist them and hold their gains for them. These developments are a strong beginning in the quest to level the playing field against corrupt actors.

MELVIN AYOGU

Non-state actors and value recovery: Ganging to create political will

Using a more encompassing terminology that denotes a multi-faceted approach to combating pillage of public resources, this paper highlights the centrality of political will in establishing a credible international regime of deterrence against grand corruption. Political will is a scarce and costly resource which contrary to popular expectation is not created by politicians. Therefore, the challenge before NSAs is to engender the required political will. One means to this end is through occupying decisively the respective domestic political space. These takeovers thus create the incentive to produce locally the necessary goods that are required internationally. How should NSAs play? Academics can offer valuable insights through research.

I. Introduction

Notwithstanding that it is an economic crime, stealing of huge quantities of public money also called 'grand corruption' clearly must be a profitable enterprise. Why else would it be so properly organised to generate an elaborate value chain that spans multiple jurisdictions; from victim countries where the crimes are perpetrated to the financial centre(s) of the world where the gains are stashed.[1] Very few people would contest the view that value recovery of stolen money is a potent deterrent against corruption, yet the near unanimity around the bene-

1 Many of the publications cited herein refer to various estimates of the magnitude of the pillage. See for instance Baker (2005), and UNODC & World Bank (2007).

fits of value recovery has not been matched universally in the supply of the level of co-operation necessary for a forceful and successful implementation of the strategy. This hypocrisy – the inconsistency in the claimed preference for anti-corruption and visible behaviour about it – exists even with the legal framework given by the UNCAC and the operational modalities contained in the StAR initiative jointly of the UNODC and the WB which altogether are meant 'to facilitate the domestication of the convention by state parties.'[2] Yet creating and sustaining international co-operation is a cross-cutting driver in the asset recovery value chain. The aim of this paper therefore, is to identify the role of NSAs in facilitating the forging of the requisite international co-operation.

As the name suggests and is used here, NSAs are the polity outside the formal organisation of government. These include civil society comprising NGOs and other organised not-for-profit segments of the society; academia including those involved in pure and applied research and knowledge management; the private sector comprising business and organised labour, political organisations, and special interest groups; media; and professional service providers (gatekeepers) who are in fact part of the private sector but are categorised separately because of the nature of their circumstances in the money laundering liability chain and AML activities spectrum. Examples of the professional service firms are technology solution providers, attorneys or civil asset recovery teams including private investigators and forensic experts; gatekeepers such as bankers, corporate lawyers, corporate service providers, trust companies, accounting and audit firms, and tax advisory.

Some of the more prominent initiatives from the private sector include the Wolfsberg Principles and PACI. With a current membership of 12 major international banks, the Wolfsberg Principles is a bankers' initiative aimed at standardising procedures on customer due diligence in private banking, and subsequently extended to counter-terrorism

2 The first global anti-corruption agreement, the UNCAC was adopted by the General Assembly resolution 58/4 of October 31, 2003 and came into force December 14, 2005. The StAR initiative is an integral part of the World Bank's Governance and Anti-Corruption Strategy whereas UNODC is both the custodian and the lead agency supporting the implementation of the UNCAC, as well as acting as the Secretariat to the Conference of State Parties.

measures and the combating of other criminal activities within the broader financial services industry. The inclusion in the Wolfsberg Principles through the subsequent establishment of guidelines on AML controls for correspondent banking relationships is remarkable because global correspondent banking is the primary mechanism for money transfers worldwide and hence is a rich repository of forensic payment information. Known as the PACI principles, representatives of leading companies from the Oil and Gas, construction and engineering, and metals and mining sectors established the foundations for corporate compliance codes to prevent bribery. Since its inauguration in 2005, the initiative now engages over 150 leaders of major companies in the implementation of zero-tolerance policy towards bribery as well as in the establishment of internal anti-corruption mechanisms.

The rest of the paper is organised as follows. Section 2 overviews the value recovery landscape and delineates the various components of the value chain. Section 3 emphasises the key drivers of each component of the value chain and highlights the criticality of international co-operation as a cross-cutting driver. Forging the requisite international co-operation is then presented as a challenge that we overcome strategically through an informed intervention that begins with formal research. Section 4 summarises and offers some suggestions on research priorities.

II. The value recovery landscape

Value recovery is a much broader concept than stolen asset recovery.[3] Its appeal lies in the recognition that victims of grand corruption can recoup their losses either through pursuing the recovery of the specific stolen assets by identifying and tracing the proceeds of the crime to

3 This section has benefitted from valuable insights gained from listening to the presentation by Edward H. Davis, Jr. in Laxenburg, Austria, September 2010, and documented in Davis and Giuliano (2010). However, all errors of understanding or interpretation are my sole responsibility.

where it is stashed and/or by pursuing claims against various parties in the liability chain. For instance, article 53 of the UNCAC is explicit on measures available for recouping the losses from embezzlement:

> Each State Party, shall in accordance with its domestic law: (…) (b) Take such measures as may be necessary to permit its courts to order those who have committed offences established in accordance with this Convention to pay compensation or damages to another State Party that has been harmed by such offences; …

Davis and Giuliano (2010) elaborate this view by noting that as victims of corruption, the customary habit of governments asking other governments for assistance in the recovery of stolen assets is constrained because such mutual assistance is ideal in circumstances where identified traceable fund or its transform can be located. By contrast, the potentially highest level of recoveries can be achieved by pursuing civil claims against all those relevant actors in the liability chain; metaphorically, going after the thief and the fence or combating all those who aid in structuring the grabbing hand to effectively strip the assets. This would include all the actors in the commission of the predicate crime as well as all those who facilitate the safe enjoyment of the benefits of the crime by concealing the proceeds of the crime. Chief among the latter would be the launderer. These authors note that although governments are not set up to pursue such civil claims themselves, nonetheless they can enlist the services of civil litigation teams to employ civil litigation devices which in combination with cooperation from state authorities can maximise value recovery of stolen public assets.

Having defined the meaning of value recovery within the context of this study, it is useful to first provide an overview of the value recovery landscape in order to meaningfully analyse the various stages of the value recovery chain as well as highlight the key drivers of each stage. Following Atkinson (2009) we categorise the value recovery landscape into four sequential stages labelled pre-investigative, investigative, judicial, and disposal. In the pre-investigative stage, the case team members (such as a forensic accountant, an investigator or both depending on the configuration of the team) assess the preliminary information to determine whether or not further action is warranted. The investigative stage is when the identification and tracing of the proceeds of the crime occurs and the facts for the case are assembled. The juridical stage is where the facts are tried, judgment is made and the applicable remedies sought and obtained. The disposal stage is when the enforcement occurs including the implementation of all the ancillary steps necessary to give effect to the order and related agreements such as mechanisms for the monitoring of the use of the recovered assets. We now turn to the analysis of each of the stages.

III. Key drivers of the value chain

Pre-investigative

Pre-investigative stage essentially creates the space for a case team to assess the likelihood of marshalling sufficient evidence to proceed with a viable litigation. In view of the complexity of a value recovery process and the resource intensity implicit, a noisy filter by way of a weak pre-investigative capability can lead to poor judgments as worthy cases are not taken up or dead-start cases are invested.[4] In fact, the importance of a pre-investigative process can be likened to the concept of market contestability in economics whereby exit costs can act as a barrier to entry and hence reduce contestability. Therefore, factors that militate against the pre-investigative process influences negatively value recovery.

Since value recovery is a composite strategy requiring the investigation as well as the prosecution of the underlying criminality (the predicate offence) and the related offence of concealing the proceeds of the crime, it is important to understand how sufficiency condition can be established in the pre-investigative stage. In view of two recent court decisions in the US on value recovery, establishing sufficiency condition has become even more relevant for decisions about initiat-

4 Part of the complexity arises from navigating across jurisdictions and within jurisdictions; and in each instance, across different law enforcement agencies. The resource intensity includes financial, physical, human, and time.

ing value recovery.[5] The two cases are relevant because they involved both money laundering and predicate offences. The decision of the Appellate Court reaffirmed and applied to a white collar crime, an earlier Supreme Court decision in *Cuellar v. US*, which ruled that concealment was insufficient to establish money laundering; it was necessary to prove that the purpose of the concealment was to 'conceal or disguise the nature, the location, the source, the ownership, or the control of the proceeds of specified unlawful activity.'[6] In this the court is said to have steered to the purpose of the money laundering laws namely to criminalise the intentional concealment of illegal monies quite independently of the predicate crime or activity that yielded the monies. ''How' one moves the money is distinct from 'why' one moves the money. Evidence of the former, standing alone, is not sufficient to prove the latter,' wrote Justice Clarence Thomas in a unanimous opinion.

In money laundering cases, a predicate crime is a necessary condition but money laundering is not necessary to establish corruption. Therefore, verification of potentially trigger information should be undertaken with regard to an allegation involving at least a predicate crime coupled with, where included, allegations of schemes to conceal illicit gains.[7] Potentially trigger information for money laundering allegations that do not link to an underlying crime from which were obtained the illegal proceeds may be difficult to sustain and can constitute a reason to demur on launching an investigation. It would be like a murder charge without a body (in a regime where a body is necessary to prove that a murder occurred). When the allegation concerns PEPs, as is likely to be the case in grand corruption, the customary apparatus of the government may not be very helpful. NSAs including the media and civil society may be the best source of initial verification. Perhaps a high sense of civic responsibility from citizens or, better yet, self-interested political elites who stand to gain from the downfall of a competitor could allow investigators to delicately test

5 US v. Faulkenberry, United States, and US v. Ayers.

6 18 U.S.C. § 1956(a)(1)B(i).

7 We introduce here and define 'trigger information' as the set of information sufficient to initiate a pre-investigative activity (sort of the critical value of a decision parameter).

some of the facts. Where the initial screening of the facts (potentially trigger information) extends beyond domestic boundaries, would bureaucrats and technocrats in foreign jurisdictions offer the necessary co-operation expeditiously? Once more, the desirability of political will is encountered.

Investigative

A successful value recovery depends largely on the strength of the evidence that the victim can provide which in turn rests on what can be discovered or proven. For this reason, the investigative stage of the process can be viewed as core to recovery efforts. To successfully frustrate this stage of the combat is to hand victory to the miscreant.

Usually the investigator in a litigation team will work closely with the forensic accountant to uncover details of the crime such as who was involved, their current whereabouts, how the crime was perpetrated, and the location of the assets. From the details, the forensic accountant develops a report containing financial information regarding transactions in connection with the crime and those relating to consequential damages. In cases of grand theft which is of primary interest here, the scope of damages is almost always understated presumably because information that speaks to the full extent of the damages unleashed by the act is not readily available.

However, this deficiency can be remedied but through a move that fully must involve NSAs. First, NSAs would have to take an active interest in foresightedly gathering forensic evidence for the prosecution and second, be prepared to learn how. The latter requires a willingness to seek greater interaction or co-operation with the relevant state authorities and experts. Prosecutors on their part can gain a great deal of support by educating and informing the appropriate segments of NSAs about the kinds of assistance and the format of admissible facts and figures required in order to successfully prosecute a case. This type of move can actually be a 'game changer.'

Since the general thrust of the analysis in this section is on incentives to supply appropriate information to generate knowledge necessary to successfully prosecute a case, the two main issues to be analysed are access to information and the introduction of a game changer. In the context of this essay, the game changer is the recommendation to expand our appreciation of damages to include what World Bank-UNODC (2007) calls collateral damages but of which we contend should instead be considered the directly foreseeable consequence of the grand embezzlement of public money. Such an attribution is plausible in the light of the order of magnitude (billions of dollars) reported as current estimates of many of the grand thefts that have come to light so far.[8] Our traditional understanding of damages and its assessment falls far short of the human developmental impact of corruption.

The developmental impact of grand corruption should be considered a direct consequential damage because human development falls within the proper scope of government. If the opportunity cost of the valuable time diverted to scheming in order to pillage is implicit in the many years of degradation of public institutions, neglect of basic infrastructure, failure to provide the proper investment climate, economic Darwinism, conflict and humanitarian emergencies, so is the opportunity cost of the stolen money explicit in the state of affairs to wit: no water, no electricity, no food, no immunisation, no ante and post natal cares, high infantile mortality, no malaria treatments, no HIV-AIDS intervention, no sanitation, no primary access roads; the list is long but the point has hopefully been made.[9] The time has come to pay proper attention to quantifying the real damages from the long years (in some cases over 30 years and in recent times up to 40 years) of cumulative deprivation and impoverishment of the citizenry particularly the poor and weak. Viewed thus, stealing the common wealth can be seen for what it truly is: the *silent killing fields*.[10]

8 World Bank and UNODC (2007), pp.8–9, 11.

9 For corroborating views, see Nafziger and Auvinen (2003).

10 The concept of recognising socioeconomic damages explicitly is similar to the initiatives underway which World Bank and UNODC (2009a) describes as the 'Human Rights' approaches to deterrence of corruption. This watershed is being tested through a collaborative venture by a Spanish human rights organisation, ADPHE, EG Justice, and OSJI (ibid, p. 47–8). Additionally, see the case of 'Elf Aquitaine and the Nigerian Construction Consortium' as well as 'Civil Party Initiation of Criminal Proceedings in France on Behalf of Cameroonians' in OSJI

With regard to access to information and incentives to disseminate or share knowledge, it will be useful to bear in mind that some of the costs of achieving value recovery are distributed across jurisdictions and interest groups whereas the distribution of the expected value (to be recovered) is concentrated across a few stipulated beneficiaries. This circumstance can generate suppressed distributional conflicts that manifest in different manners including infighting by government agencies, apathy from requested jurisdictions or delays and inaction from States Parties. For instance, two of the G8 members (which within such a small grouping add up to a non-trivial proportion of the membership) have not ratified UNCAC after seven years of the adoption of the resolution, and five years of its entering into force. To a first approximation, non-ratification of the Convention is instructive in its implications for readiness to facilitate access to information. Articles 26, 40, 43, and 52 of UNCAC altogether largely enjoins and in most of the instances make it obligatory for states parties to the UNCAC to co-operate and to ensure that bank secrecy laws do not obstruct domestic criminal investigation of criminal offences covered under the Convention. Given that many of the financial centres which become final repositories of the stolen monies or act as conduits thereof are located in the developed world, Article 26 which requires states parties to establish the criminal, civil, or administrative liability of juristic person's complicity in predicate crimes is of note. The point being that the political economy circumstances which drive the undermining of compliance with any of the steps mandated by the above articles is appreciated even if disappointing.

In the discovery process, injunctive relief or pre-judgment remedies (also known as interim civil measures) are crucial to the endeavour. In some cases, failure to secure a freeze order timely can amount to 'winning the battle but losing the war' given that the end goal is to clearly demonstrate that the enterprise of grand corruption is not profitable. If criminals become judgment-proof by cleverly parting with the property before judgment, it will indeed be a travesty of justice.

(2005). Besides, quantifying damages is also pertinent in terms of Article 57 of UNCAC which requires return of confiscated property upon reasonable establishment of prior ownership or recognition of damage [Art. 57, para. 3b].

Domestication of the UNCAC can be facilitative of injunctive relief by providing (as a signaling value) the right atmosphere within which the judicial authorities of states parties can predispose to avail prosecutors of civil interim measures variously within their dispensation.

Without doubt, the challenges faced in discovery (access problems) can be adequately managed within the existing arrangements as delineated within the UNCAC legal framework and operational modalities of StAR initiatives. The problem is that their (the framework and modalities) functionality is underpinned by political will that is yet to be delivered. Why the political will has not been created and how it can be engendered is what this paper suggests to be the primary goal which ought to preoccupy NSAs and to which their resources should also be gainfully deployed.

Having reviewed the literature on the various technical hurdles and challenges which confront litigators in the value recovery process, it is tempting to recommend that all the NSAs join the foray and help in one way or the other so as to overcome the problem created by ignorance or lack of resources. That would miss the point and steer the energy in the wrong trajectory. As has been made abundantly clear in the literature, an understanding of the challenges or knowledge of what-to-do (i.e., action plan) is not the issue.[11]

Specifically, the issue is not what to do with international business corporations, trusts, secrecy jurisdictions, and 'gatekeepers' or how to do make them open up or co-operate with legitimate investigations within the UNCAC framework. It is a matter of whether states parties, mindful of the costs in political capital, will go the distance? To return assets means to deprive someone else of a resource. From a purely redistributive perspective, for one state party to confiscate or regain assets represents a loss to another state party independently of the value judgment. Because of the *status quo* bias and the inertia it generates, consideration should be given to a discussion of the costs of socialising the reforms or adjustment and whether it would be worth

11 Readers can consult World Bank & UNODC (2007), UNODC (1998), World Bank & UNODC (2011), World Bank & UNODC (2009a), World Bank & UNODC (2009b), UNCAC 2003, Murphy (2011), Basel Institute on Governance (2008), and ICAR (2009).

the present value of the expected future benefits of deterring grand corruption. That is part of the calculus that NSAs would want to engage and of which the academia is well suited. Such considerations also offer one more reason for wanting to quantify the damages from 'stealing the commonwealth.'

Juridical

All the preparations come to a head at the trail stage during which the allegations are tested, in accordance with the applicable law, against the facts in evidence. In short, this is the point at which the facts are tried according to the relevant burden of proof. Then, judgment is rendered as to whether or not to forfeit or confiscate as the case may be. Recalling an earlier example from the economics of industry which was used to emphasise how high exit costs can be a barrier to entry and thus can be viewed as anti-competitive, similarly it can be shown that protracted legal proceedings can be an inhibitor of value recovery by raising entry costs or correspondingly overall participation costs. Consequently, it can be viewed as an anti-deterrent. For this reason, this section focuses on ways of reducing the overall costs of pursuing value recovery (i.e., efficiency of the juridical process).

Analysis and recommendations from the literature suggest that standardisation by way of harmonisation and codification of the relevant laws can enhance efficiency. The groundwork for such harmonisation and codification (and initiatives around the introduction of model legislation) has already been laid under the framework of UNCAC.[12] Although the framework is not perfect in addressing all the evolving challenges in the value recovery landscape, it is nonetheless the most comprehensive legal framework for international co-operation and it has over the last seven years proved to be dynamic and capable of interfacing with other ancillary initiatives such a FATF

12 Legislative reforms including crafting of model laws within the ambit of the United Nations are on-going initiatives to improve efficiency of MLA and mitigate impediments that derive from navigating issues across multi jurisdictions. See discussions in UNODC (1998), pp. 104–6, and World Bank & UNODC (2009b).

and StAR in order to advance both technical and policy issues.[13] In this regard, a fundamental push would be for nations to domesticate the articles of the convention as a concrete step in achieving harmonisation of technical issues some of which now delay processes. As noted earlier, predisposition to dispense pre-judgment remedies can be facilitated by domestication of the convention. Evidently, domestication of the articles is a cross-cutting driver. Again, this goal like all the other desirable objectives noted in the preceding analyses is underpinned by political will.[14]

Furthermore, capacity building and continuing professional education on a multi-stakeholder basis would be useful. Law should talk to neighboring sciences in order to improve the quality of support and evidence that it can access. Without a good understanding of the 'pain points' in the processes, the quality of support that can be delivered by NSAs is bound to lie below its full capabilities.

Repatriation

Without doubt, value recovery is a very resource intensive process. Therefore, it is understandable for stakeholders to be concerned over some of the more visible benefits of such humongous investment. One such major concern is the revolving door syndrome according to which returned assets are pillaged once more – effectively revolved

13 FATF is the standard setter in the global AML regime particularly the preventive aspects.

14 To appreciate the influence of international co-operation (good will) on the course of juridical processes, consider that in one of first cases of asset recovery, the Philippine case against Ferdinand Marcos, took eighteen years to conclude whereas subsequent cases such as Peru and Nigeria against Montesinos and Abacha respectively took a maximum of five years. More to the point is the fact that Swiss authorities were relatively more liberal in imposing a general freezing order in these subsequent processes. In the case against Montesinos, the freezing order had been proactively issued by the Swiss authorities even before a formal request from Peruvian authorities [see, World Bank & UNODC (2007), p.24]. A similar proactive stance has been taken by the Swiss authorities with regard to Hosni Mubarak's alleged loot [Rohde and Roston (2011)], and by the Swiss, Belgian and Canadian authorities with regard to Ben Ali of Tunisia [Thanh Ha (2011)].

out of the back door to international financial centres. This highly likely prospect of turning value recovery into a Sisyphean labour is worrying to investors (in value recovery). Therefore, the analysis in this section focuses on addressing such abiding concern.

According to John Stoessinger, the relevance of the Sisyphean myth to modern world politics is clear.

> In many respects, modern man has descended to unprecedented depths yet in others he has soared to greater heights than ever before. (…) We may never solve the problems of our human condition – in international relations or in anything else – completely and permanently. But what remains crucial for us, as it was for Sisyphus, is that we do not permit our rock to crush us.[15]

Asset repatriation is a resource flow that can contribute to servicing a nation's debts, to developmental goals and to the reimbursement of the resource cost of value recovery (litigation expenses and all incidentals thereof). The mechanism design to ensure that this happens is well covered in most of the volumes on asset recovery that have been cited here. Furthermore, NSAs have also continued to engage in this connection.

The final point of interest with regard to the fate of the recovered value is to emphasise that even in the extreme case of no feasible mechanism which ensures that recovered value will be husbanded once repatriated, a solution around that failure can be devised by allowing the value to remain in trust with the requested country or some other acceptable preservation trust. Never should the fate of recovered money be the basis for failing to pursue value recovery with all available vigor. To do so would be to miss the principal reason for value recovery: its value as a deterrent. So long as the criminal does not benefit from the crime, distributional issues around the recovered loot remain auxiliary. Besides, rationality of organised crime leads society to conclude that even to contemplate and then sink the observed scale of investment in money laundering infrastructure then, it must be the case that the present discounted expected future benefits of eliminating grand corruption necessarily exceed the net value of current recoveries.

15 Stoessinger (1979), p. 4–5.

IV. Summary and concluding remarks

Hopefully the contribution of this essay to the body of knowledge on value recovery goes beyond a restatement of the obvious: the centrality of international co-operation (political goodwill) in deterring embezzlement. The general lack of political will to implement a universally worthy cause is understandable although regrettable. Political will is a scarce resource and does not come free; it is very costly. Since political will is not created by politicians, the challenge before NSAs is to engender the requisite political will; to decisively occupy the respective domestic political space in order to produce locally the necessary goods that are required internationally. How should NSAs play?

By first encouraging academics to work in concurrence with researchers imbedded in many of the NGOs (on the latter, see for instance, UNODC (2009a), p.52) so as to assist in identifying the nature of incentives that confront politicians. Clearly what is at stake is political but the problem in view is economic. The difficulty in attempting to forge the kind of international co-operation envisaged here is that such co-operation is in the nature of providing a public benefit (foreign policy). Provision of a public good generates conflicts over the distribution of the costs of supplying the good. When a policy has distributional consequences, self-interested groups will be in conflict. This conflict represents a form of political constraint that can lead to either delays in the adoption or the non-adoption of seemingly beneficial policies. Then, the challenge is to understand how these political constraints can be overcome within existing institutional frameworks (i.e., prevailing collective choice mechanisms).

References

Atkinson, Phyllis (2009) 'Introduction' in *Tracing Stolen Assets: A Practitioner's Handbook.* Basel Switzerland: International Centre for Asset Recovery, Basel Institute on Governance, p. 19–22.

Baker, Raymond W. (2005) *Capitalism's Achilles Heel: Dirty Money and How to Renew the Free-Market System.* New Jersey: John Wiley & Sons.

Basel Institute on Governance (2008) *Recovering Stolen Asset.* Ed. Mark Pieth. Bern: Peter Lang.

Cuellar v. U.S. #06-1456, Supreme Court of United States, 2007

Davis, Edward H. & Douglas J. Giuliano (2010) 'Leveling the Playing Field: The use of civil litigation to locate and recover assets misappropriate through corruption.' Paper presented at the conference of Non-State Actors in the Asset Recovery Processes, hosted by Basel Institute on Governance & International Anti-Corruption Academy, Laxenburg, Austria, 2–3 September 2010.

International Centre for Asset Recovery (2009) *Tracing Stolen Assets: A Practitioner's Handbook.* Basel: ICAR, Basel Institute on Governance.

Murphy, Richard (2011) 'Jersey claims this is tax information exchange' in Task Force on Financial Integrity & Economic Development, accessed 18 January 2011. http://www.financialtaskforce.org/2011/01/18/jersey-claims-this-is-tax-information-exchange/.

Nafziger E. Wayne, and Juha Auvinen (2003) 'Chapter1: A Humanitarian Emergency: War, Genocide, and Displacement' in *Economic Development, Inequality, and War: Humanitarian emergencies in Developing Countries.* New York: Palgrave Macmillan, pp. 1–29.

Open Society Justice Initiative (2005), *Legal Remedies for the Resource Curse: A digest of experience using law to combat natural resource corruption.* New York: Open Society Institute.

Rohde, David, and Aram Roston (2011) 'Assets of Mubarak and aides are frozen by Swiss' *New York Times*, accessed 19 February 2011. http://www.ndtv.com/article/world/assets-of-mubarak-and-aides-are-frozen-by-swiss-86471.

Stoessinger, John G. (1979) *The Might of Nations: World Politics in Our Time*. 6th Edition, New York: Random House.

Thanh Ha, Tu (2011) 'Kleptocrats: The dictator's guide to amassing wealth,' *The Globe And Mail*, Tuesday March 1, 2011. Accessed 3 March 2011, http://www.theglobeandmail.com/news/world/kleptocrats-the-dictators-guide-to-amassing-wealth/article 1926083/page1/.

United Nations Convention Against Corruption (2003) [UNCAC] *United Nations, Treaty Series*, vol.2349, p.41 Doc.A/58/442. http://treaties.un.org/.

United Nations Office for Drug Control and Crime (1998) 'Financial Havens, Banking Secrecy and Money Laundering' Ed: Jack A. Blum, Michael Levi, Thomas Naylor and Phil Williams. Monograph prepared by on behalf of the UN under auspices of the Global Programme Against Money Laundering, Office for Drug Control and Crime Prevention. Accessed 18 February 2011, http://siteresources.worldbank.org/.

U.S. v. Ayers, #08-4166 and 08-4405, United States Court of Appeals, 2010.

U.S. v. Faulkenberry, #08-4233 and 08-4404, United States Court of Appeals, 2010.

18 U.S.C. Sec 1956 (a) (1) B (i).

World Bank and United Nations Office for Drug Control and Crime (2007) *Stolen Asset Recovery (StAR) Initiative: Challenges, Opportunities, and Action Plan*, Washington, DC: The World Bank

(2009a) *Stolen Asset Recovery: Towards a Global Architecture for Asset Recovery* UNCAC Conference Edition. Accessed 18 February 2011, http://siteresources.worldbank.org/.

(2009b) *Stolen Asset Recovery: A Good Practices Guide for Non-Conviction Based Asset Forfeiture* Ed: Theodore S. Greenberg, Linda M. Samuel, Wingate Grant, and Larissa Gray on behalf of Stolen Asset Recovery (StAR) Initiative. Washington, DC: The World Bank.

(2011) *Asset Recovery Handbook: A Guide for Practitioners* Ed: Jean-Pierre Brun, Larissa Gray, Clive Scott, and Kevin M. Stephenson on behalf of the Stolen Asset Recovery Initiative. Washington, DC: The World Bank.

MAX MADER

Civil society facilitators of asset recovery. The two Swiss cases Mobutu and Abacha

I. Abstract

Experience shows that NSAs can substantially contribute to asset recovery. This article describes the Abacha and Mobutu cases. It analyses the major benefits and challenges of NSA contributions and of coordination with state and international actors. – The most important findings are that there is no such thing as a country of origin's stable 'political will' either to recover or not to recover its stolen assets. Rather, there is a balance of interests of domestic politics which duly considered can be altered in favour of recovery for a limited time. Furthermore, negotiating authorities of receiving countries tend to underestimate how NSA facilitation can create democratic legitimacy of promoters of asset recovery within the country of origin and – hence – quickly resolve the issue of sovereignty within bilateral negotiations.

As the purpose of this article is to give some practical considerations on asset recovery, it will detail out even quite simple means for achieving some important tasks specific to NSA's commitment in asset recovery.

* This article is dedicated to Yoav Parish, an old friend and amused listener to asset recovery stories. The author acknowledges the open-mindedness of his governmental and institutional partners as well as the strong support of local, international and Swiss civil society colleagues. They helped forging and implementing new ideas more swiftly than in normal politics.

II. Introduction

The process of asset recovery can be conceived in three stages. The case material presented here concerns less the stage of discovery and freezing, but rather the two later stages of negotiations and of repatriation. This is due to obvious limitations of access to the legal proceedings NSAs, as they are normally not legal party to requests for MLA or to legal proceedings. The cases reflect Switzerland's strong diplomatic approach to asset recovery. In other countries, the judicial authorities lead the process of asset recovery. In most Swiss cases, the FDFA negotiates as the authority in charge during a certain period with ministries, international or multilateral bodies, according to specific needs. This facilitates the exchange of information between NSAs and Swiss authorities, as the diplomatic actors are less bound by legal secrecy requirements and have an active interest in receiving external information in exchange for 'hints' they give. Consequently, it remains open if this 'Swiss experience' can be transferred to other countries' policies on asset recovery. The UK's policy in this field might be seen as similar to Switzerland's, insofar as DfID co-finances the investigative authorities' stolen asset case investigations.

III. Civil society's 'resource privilege'

All three stages of asset recovery pose a problem of limited capacities to the authorities of both the country of origin of the stolen assets and the one receiving them. During the first stage, namely detecting and freezing, embassies of recipient countries have only limited resources to monitor and forward information to their money laundering reporting offices. In contrast, NGOs constantly receive information through their local networks and monitor the media in the countries of origin.

This problem of limited capacities can lead to the withdrawal by the money launderer of the stolen assets before they can be frozen.

Therefore, an immediate response to potential cases is crucial. In the case of Noele and Salim, two former directors of Indonesian commercial banks, Swiss NGOs forwarded media clippings to the Swiss authorities which lead, in February 2008, to the freezing of accounts within 6 days.

As the following will show, this 'resource privilege' is even more important during the negotiations and the repatriation of stolen assets.

Mobutu – Information and diplomacy

Only in December 2008 would the Government in Kinshasa decide to recover Mobutu's stolen assets, 11 years after its first request for MLA. The in-between period was characterised by thwarted attempts from the Swiss Government to give every possible technical support to the local authorities and to obtain sufficient evidence and a formal declaration of political will from the DRC. However, as Nzanga-Mobutu, Sese Seko's eldest son, had become part of the Government, there was a trade-off between opening proceedings against the Mobutu heirs and waiving the Government's claim to the funds; this policy of conciliation with the UDEMO moderated the Government's activism considerably. Consequently, Swiss diplomacy and judiciary neither succeeded in finding political support for the recovery nor in obtaining the necessary evidence during this decade.

In 2007 and 2008, Switzerland undertook in vain the last efforts to motivate Kinshasa to submit a formal declaration of will. By the end of November 2008 the situation seemed clearly hopeless. That was when NSAs stepped in.

IV. Establishing a network

Against recommendations to drop this lost case, the author succeeded in funding a 10-day mandate to travel to Kinshasa and see what could be done. As a facilitator working on-site, the first step taken was building a network with the local NGOs working on the case; national, parliamentary and church organisations; the Swiss Embassy; as well as the World Bank and the UN offices in both Kinshasa and Washington, DC. While these actors would become involved in more or less active roles according to their interest and sensitivities, they became all part of a network, choosing either from a mutual exchange of information or just to receive them. The Congolese government agencies were not direct parties of the network, but were linked to it through the local and national NGOs and the Swiss Embassy in Kinshasa, all of which had the necessary political legitimacy to act. This construct allowed regular estimates on salient questions. As such, if any progress on the recovery of assets were to be possible, it would be necessary to find out the position taken by different government authorities concerning the Mobutu funds, and if there were agencies inclined to request for the return of the funds, apart from what the official statements had so far indicated. Consequently, establishing the network was, in practice, what theorists of asset recovery call 'identifying champions of asset recovery' within the country of origin, which is estimated as a central task for the asset recovery process.

The network is best established in gradual steps, i.e., first it is prepared and communicated before travelling on-site. This requires one or two day's phone calls to all chosen partners, which is the best way to introduce ideas and convince people who don't yet know it, but are willing and in a position to implement the idea. The idea of identifying and supporting champions of asset recovery on-site is, again, very simple, but needs some elaboration on its implementation and purpose to become compelling. Namely, it is worth emphasizing that once these champions are found, they will act immediately within the government, in co-ordination with foreign embassies, multilateral or international institutions, and backed up by the lobbying of local and national NGOs and through the media. The quintessence of this is that due to the 'champions' participation this new network has a high potential to substantially change the present situation.

The important advantage of this preparatory step is that, independently of the actual support of the idea by the addressed people, no resources have been wasted so far and there is a basis for deciding to travel or to drop the case. If there is positive response, it makes sense to notify media contacts in the receiving country, as this will create public support of its embassy's further commitment in the case.

Both the Swiss authorities and Congolese NGOs gave their immediate and full support and agreed to talk on a daily basis or to meet according to needs.

The second step is to get in touch with the network partners once on-site and to arrange planning meetings with the core partners. Informal meetings at the hotel lobby are the only viable way of face-to-face meetings under time constraints; clearly, phone calls are no alternative for planning and co-ordinating joint activities of a group, apart from the fact that one wants to know, i.e. meet and see one's partner. However, bilateral phone updates are indispensable in order to keep actions well co-ordinated, as the following sub-chapter shows.

The main NGO contact persons came to the author's hotel lobby several times for planning and evaluation. The only 'external' meetings that had to be organised were a discussion with the Swiss Ambassador and three meetings with the NGOs dealing with the Mobutu case, development and church NGOs and the umbrella NGOs with official parliamentary status.

V. Civil society's 'ticker service'

When aiming at finding promoters of asset recovery within the government, the backbone of the established network are immediate updates on important new developments. This includes emails for information that is less urgent, but important to receive for the wider network, as well as phone calls for urgent information to core partners when also action may be needed. In practical terms, this also means working in the hotel room with a WLAN and a local mobile phone rather than sneaking out to meetings.

This 'ticker service' establishes the facilitator from NSA as an informant in assisting decision makers and diplomats to become fast movers who are slightly ahead of their government interlocutors. It puts them in a position not only to identify 'champions of asset recovery', but also to link them up on the several government levels, from the lower authorities to cabinet.

The main feed of information from the author to the Swiss Embassy contained updates on the NGOs' media and lobbying activities, and from the author to the NGOs, the Swiss Embassy's hints on their activities with several Congolese Ministries, cabinet meetings etc. Either feeds allowed the actors to time their interventions well and to contact the right Congolese government agencies.

VI. Media work

Accompanying media coverage of the on-site developments strengthens the diplomatic interventions, because in the receiving country it demonstrates that something is being done; in the country of origin it creates an atmosphere of democratic legitimacy.

Phone calls with Swiss media contacts and media work in Kinshasa served as 'Swiss media back-up'. In Kinshasa, the local NGOs organised the media contributions with financial contributions of Swiss NGOs, as the Congolese media take 'distribution fees' in order to pay the journalists' salaries. A radio interview at Radio Okapi, the UN channel, and 5 press articles held the public debate alive during the negotiations of the Congolese and Swiss authorities.

VII. Lobbying on-site

NSA facilitators of the receiving country or from international NGOs must never take an active role in lobbying government or parliamentary authorities of the country of origin. As foreigners, they lack all legitimacy to do so. Only the NGOs of the country of origin can achieve this task. However, it never hurts if facilitators support them in every useful way in the background.

The core group of NGOs in Kinshasa met Nzanga-Mobutu's secretary on 10 December 2008 and promoted the idea of a government that would proactively set a signal of commitment to transparency that would benefit the country's international image. The author declined the NGOs' invitation to attend the meeting, declaring that he was acting as a facilitator and resource person on-site. Obviously, his presence as promoter of a policy change that is directed against the Congolese conciliatory policy with the Mobutu heirs could have been perceived as an affront.

VIII. Shifting the balance of political interests

At the end of a week's diplomacy, the Minister of Justice, together with Prime Minister Alphonse Muzito, managed in a cabinet meeting to arbitrate the consent of Mobutu on the Government's request for asset recovery. On 12 December 2008, President Kabila submitted a formal mandate to a Swiss lawyer to open criminal proceedings against the Mobutu heirs.

This success against all odds was acknowledged in Switzerland with a mixture of perplexity and deep satisfaction that the existing lacunas of Swiss law would not have the feared effect of letting the perpetrators get away with impunity. The fact that they unfortunately had this effect during the subsequent proceedings and that the Mobutu heirs are now in possession of the stolen assets still allows to draw conclusions from the success story of December 2008 for NSA practice.

Clearly, the Swiss government's perception, until November 2008, that Kinshasa lacked the political will for asset recovery was flawed, because it relied exclusively on official statements. Progress was possible once it started obtaining differing positions from different Congolese government agencies. Identifying 'champions of asset recovery' within these agencies has shown to be the core tool for countries receiving stolen assets in order to motivate countries of origin to request asset recovery, even against opposing interests of domestic policy.

NSAs, on the other hand, misconceived the Mobutu case as a lost case. It regained ground by virtue of creating a fast moving network on-site for a very limited time, thereby triggering the diplomatic agencies' search and support for 'champions of asset recovery'.

Consequently, 'the' political will of a country of origin is susceptible and not just given. The objection that this conception compromises the principle of sovereignty is flawed, because it equally takes the official statements as the only position of the government of origin. Rather, the policy of governments of receiving countries and of NSAs should be to help local and national NGOs of countries of origin as well as its government agencies in promoting asset recovery against official opposition and incrimination. In other words, both actors can and should influence in order to guarantee that the right people on the ground are no longer kept from taking influence.

IX. Personal security – A refugee case

The criminal claim against the Mobutus caused outrage within the UDEMO; party representatives saw a breach of the conciliation policy. When the Swiss judicial authorities dismissed the claim based on statutes of limitations in April 2009, fears arose that a witch-hunt against 'the culprits' would start. In June 2009, the Congolese security forces detained journalists and members of the International Red Cross, stating that, 'foreign elements want to destabilise the Congolese Government'. Within this campaign also human rights activists were summoned and interrogated.

One core NGO contact person in the Mobutu case who had been working with Kinshasa district police departments on cases of arbitrary detainments and forced disappearances was summoned several times. When he stopped following suit to the summons out of fear of arbitrary detainment, the Presidential Guard searched his house and took away the family's passports. The family started to live in clandestine accommodations. An elder uncle was arrested in the contact person's residence and disappeared. A barrister friend failed to find the uncle when visiting several jails; a sister managed to fly to South Africa. – In November 2009, the contact person's name appeared on two orders of arrest, from the Presidential Guard and from the National Police, stating as reason for arrest 'conspiracy against and destabilisation of the Government'. Subsequently, the entire family lived on the move, shifting from a secret dwelling to another every few nights.

In June 2010, the political situation worsened when the National Police shot a human rights activist the Swiss embassy had been working with. The family of the contact person later split up for security reasons and lived in Kinshasa's secret hotels that offer anonymity and a security arrangement at a cost. The Swiss NGOs financed these hotel stays and facilitated the family's request for political refugee status in Switzerland. The FOM granted immigration for further consideration of the request. However, as the Presidential Guard had seized the passports, leaving the country was a challenge. Furthermore, travelling under the real name would imply the danger of arrest. The Swiss NGOs activated the existing network in Kinshasa to seek a solution and in November 2010, the family travelled on two separate itineraries and arrived safely in Switzerland.

NSAs is clearly vulnerable in their engagement in asset recovery, as this case shows. This may not be virulent to the same degree in work environments other than Kinshasa, where the NGOs are smaller and fragmented than elsewhere, thus making individuals much more exposed to criminalisation, harassment and state violence. Obviously, there are very simple precautions; a group or organisation being responsible is always better than individuals. As the following section on the Abacha case shows, activists organised in a broad coalition need to fear much less becoming a target of arbitrary political repression and threats.

It is clear that NGOs would profit enormously of training material on how to minimise security exposure. Other NSAs in asset recovery who have this kind of knowledge may, in turn, profit from NGO networks on-site that are trained to act without putting themselves in unnecessary danger. Specifically, as the conference on which this reader is based has clearly shown, forensic investigators benefit from 'civil investigators', i.e. NGO members of local networks who can – without raising suspicions, as they are locals – collect and document evidence that meets the requirements of a lawsuit.[1]

Abacha – negotiating bipartite monitoring

The recovery of the Abacha funds, frozen in Switzerland in 2006, was a landmark case. It was the world's first asset recovery that was combined with a monitoring of the utilisation of the funds after their recovery. The idea of monitoring came from NSAs and at first caused fierce opposition from the Nigerian Government. In the end, a bipartite monitoring scheme was negotiated and two teams of 10 government and NSA members, respectively, were formed and trained. They conducted field inspections, accountability file checks, both combined with interviews. Two independent reports were written, one by the World Bank, who was responsible for the monitoring of the returned assets, and another by the NSA participants, whose scope was its own findings and interpretations – which differed partially from the WB's monitoring, as well as to ensure democratic checks and balances to the monitoring. Both reports coincided in their findings, but assessed their use differently. The summary facts were that out of the 53[2] projects that the returned assets had been earmarked for, 29 had been abandoned, were not functional or not staffed, according to the NGO Shadow Report, summarised at the end of this chapter.

1 The author has been promoting the idea of training material or workshops on investigation techniques, collecting and documenting proper evidence as well as personal security measures for civil society members.

2 Stated sample sizes differ, as the WB and the NGO Shadow Report include respectively exclude projects where access to project sites and project information was partly inaccessible.

X. A clear cut case with much to loose

The Abacha funds, frozen on Swiss bank accounts, amounted to around USD 500 million, a relevant sum for projects in public service and infrastructure. Furthermore, the Swiss courts had stated the criminal origin of the funds. Therefore, it was possible to apply a paragraph of the Swiss law on mutual legal assistance that allows for repatriating the funds before the legal proceedings have been terminated. In August 2004, the FOJ decided to repatriate the assets.

However, the Nigerian and Swiss NSAs raised serious concerns with regard to this so-called early repatriation. They feared that the assets would again disappear after their recovery instead of being used for developing infrastructure and public services in Nigeria. They recalled that TI's CPI had rated Nigeria very poorly. Namely, Nigeria received only 2 of 10 points, 10 describing the lowest perception of corruption, and was the second to last on the CPI country list.[3]

Furthermore, in another large Swiss case of asset recovery, the Marcos funds, the outcome had not been satisfactory. According to the Swiss Federal Supreme Court's decision in 1997, the Philippines had to inform Switzerland on a regular basis about the progress in using the repatriated funds for compensation of the victims of human rights violations during the Marcos regime.[4] However, since this decision, the Philippine Parliament had passed not even the Compensation Act, and the Philippine media reported that in 2004 President Aquino had embezzled part of the returned funds for election campaigns.

XI. Sovereignty and corruption – The 'image policy' point

When the Abacha funds were to be repatriated, Switzerland's asset recovery policy was still categorical about the sovereignty issue.

3 http://www.transparency.de/uploads/media/04-10-20_CPI_2004_DEU.pdf, p. 2, 9.

4 Swiss Supreme Court, decision of December 10, 1997 BGE 123 II 595.

However, this implied the danger of 'stolen asset recycling', i.e., the reappearance of recovered money on Swiss bank accounts – obviously a result that would cause disastrous image effects to Switzerland.

To lead a way out of this impasse, Swiss NGOs lobbied the Swiss negotiators and recalled that Article 184 of the Constitution mandates the Swiss government to 'safeguard the international image of Switzerland' and, therefore, offers a legal basis for diplomatic initiative.

The meetings showed, however, that the several Swiss authorities were only to various degrees susceptible to this line of argument. The insight was poorly established that two conflicting interests, namely the respect for Nigeria's sovereignty and due consideration of its high degree of corruption, needed urgent attention. More would be necessary to enable a policy shift.

XII. Creating democratic legitimacy

Respecting the sovereignty of the country in which the stolen assets originate, during their recovery, remains a challenge. While it is necessary to ensure that the money does not disappear again, it must be the country of origin that should decide how this is guaranteed. Prior, but also parallel to the questions of technical assistance that arise from this situation, there is a need to build the political will for such monitoring exercise.

As a rule, countries of origin are reluctant to accept the idea of monitoring the use of the returned assets and of the participation of non-state actors in such monitoring, on the one hand, because within bilateral negotiations this can appear to have a neo-colonialist interference, and on the other, because national NSAs is generally not yet seen as a more or less well accepted lobbying partner. NSAs should, therefore, create some pressure in favour of its participation in such monitoring. This is best done by virtue of building a representative coalition, representative meaning registered with Parliament as some umbrella NGOs are, having a broad constituency as trade unions do, guaranteeing a balanced regional representation or the participation of the full variety of relevant types of organisations, i.e. faith-based, trade union, human rights, development, environmental etc. It is also important to have facilitating agencies as supporters. Namely, regional desks of foreign development services have an active interest in supporting democratisation initiatives of local NGOs.

In October 2004, the Swiss NGO coalition working on the Abacha case decided to mobilise Nigerian NSAs and sent a three-member delegation to Nigeria, among which was also the author. Nigerian NGOs had invited Nigerian and Swiss government representatives to a founding conference of the Nigerian Civil Society Network on Stolen Assets under the headline 'What to do with 500 Million Abacha funds'. In their presence, the use of such funds for development projects and the monitoring of these funds were discussed. During the three-day conference, the Nigerian NGOs elected a steering committee that represented the six geopolitical regions of Nigeria and a national co-ordinator.

As a next practical step, the existence of a representative NSA coalition should be made public, promoting the ideas and line of argument it represents with core lobbying partners. This will strengthen the negotiating position of the receiving country and make the policy alternative an option for the country of origin. Indeed, the latter must be convinced that the suggested policy alternative is in the best national interest. With some luck, it will then adopt the policy alternative as its own idea. NSA's task here is no less than selling a double bed to the pope and convincing him that it was his own idea to buy it.

In a Swiss and international media release during the conference, the Swiss NGO delegation communicated the founding of the Nigerian CSO Network with its concerns and requests; the Network did the same and requested Switzerland's help in guaranteeing that the money would be used as intended. The Swiss authorities found this media work helpful for their negotiations with Nigeria, as they could now base their suggestions on requests from Nigerian citizens, i.e., on Nigerian domestic politics.

As already stated for the Mobutu case, the initiative and ownership in lobbying government or parliamentary authorities should always be with NSA organisations of the country of origin, for obvious reasons of democratic legitimacy of any requests made at the meeting.

If foreign NSA facilitators accompany them to meetings or not, it will depend on the needs of the local NGOs. As a rule, facilitators from the receiving country should be very cautious in attending meetings with representatives of the country of origin.

Upon request, the Swiss NGO delegation accompanied the Nigerian Network to meetings in Parliament and participated in the founding conference of the Network where the Nigerian Government was also represented. The Network's purpose was to demonstrate the interest of its Swiss counterparts to assist in finding a safe way to recover the assets, as 'Switzerland also has an image to lose', if the funds disappear again. The strategy was successful, probably because it created additional transparency about the involved actors.

XIII. Embassy lobbying

NSA facilitators from the receiving country should use their embassies or similar agencies as their main partner for exchange and joint initiatives, because they have the legitimacy to act on-site and to negotiate with the country of origin. Furthermore, the superiors they report to at home must be part of the network of exchange in advance of any work on the ground, as they make the political decisions and need to be interested in and supportive of NSA's activities on the ground. While this is normally the case due to long-term work relationships between NGOs with government authorities, it is important and needs to be mentioned.

Within this network, the embassies can promote policy alternatives with the country of origin and support the local NGOs requests. It is clear that embassies should be briefed by virtue of phone conversations and not just emails, as they are core partners on the ground and need to get an impression about whom they are going to deal with.

Before travelling to Abuja, the Swiss delegation briefed the authority in charge in Berne and the Swiss Ambassador to Nigeria, requesting a meeting at the embassy in Abuja to further discuss the best strategy for NSA support of the monitoring idea. It had become clear that the FDFA was in favour of the monitoring and shared the view that improving the international transparency image may be an policy option for Nigeria, especially so, because the Nigerian Finance Minister Ngozi Okonjo-Iweala, a former World Bank staff, promoted a new transparency policy for Nigeria.

XIV. Informal meeting with the Nigerian Minister of Finance in Davos

In January 2005, the national co-ordinator of the Nigerian Civil Society Network on Stolen Assets attended the WEF in Davos. He and three members of the Swiss NGO coalition met Ngozi Okonjo-Iweala to discuss the utilisation and monitoring of the Abacha funds. The fact that the Abacha money was already utilised through domestic borrowing in 2004 in anticipation of the recovery of the funds had raised concerns both with the Swiss Government and Nigerian and Swiss NSAs that no new projects would be financed, but only disbursement arrears of completed projects be paid for.

As expected, Okonjo-Iweala pointed out the sovereignty problem with regard to the suggested monitoring. It became obvious that the negotiations with Switzerland and the WB had not yet led to Nigeria accepting the monitoring. NSA members suggested to Okonjo-Iweala the idea that a monitoring exercise with NGO participation would boost Nigeria's transparency image both in domestic and international politics and, thus, attract FDI.

XV. Monitoring expertise and financing

Swiss authorities remained cautious about which party should organise and manage the monitoring, Swiss agencies being too small to achieve this task for the given project amount. Instead, they looked for an international or multilateral institution that could manage the monitoring. The WB was their first choice because of existing relations with the Nigerian Minister of Finance.

Given the challenging environment, NSAs requested both physical and financial monitoring, i.e., checks, if the projects existed and to what degree they were implemented as well as if the amounts earmarked were disbursed or if there was overpricing that would hint to corruption.

In the end of 2005, the Swiss NGOs provided a list of 32 Swiss monitoring professionals as well as of Nigerian NSA members with experience in project monitoring. The list was submitted both to the Swiss authorities and to the country responsible for economic policy of the WB with whom a close exchange continued until the publication of the monitoring report. First, the organisation, staffing and financing of the monitoring was discussed. The NGOs suggested 10 representatives who had experience in monitoring development projects, of which four were steering committee members of the Nigerian Civil Society Network on Stolen Assets and the rest of professional development organisations, e.g. Action Aid International. Public credibility of the monitoring exercise benefited from this broad regional and professional NSA participation, as a purely government-staffed team would have been perceived with some scepticism, given the mixed record of Nigerian transparency policy.

Furthermore, the NGOs received financing from the Heinrich Boell Foundation's Nigerian office in order to cover all costs of their participation in the monitoring.

XVI. Civil society participation as credibility factor

The Nigerian Civil Society Network on Stolen Assets, with support of the Swiss NGOs, kept promoting the idea of a bipartite monitoring that would create credibility both in domestic and international politics. Although the WB criticised the pressure the NGOs mounted in order to obtain what they wanted, in the end a bipartite monitoring with 10 Nigerian government and 10 NSA representatives was agreed between Nigeria, Switzerland and the WB.[5]

On 27 September 2005, the WB President Paul Wolfowitz, Nigerian Finance Minister Ngozi Okonjo-Iweala and Swiss Secretary of State Jean-Daniel Gerber announced the planned monitoring exercise in a video teleconference at the WB headquarters.

XVII. Two one-week monitoring exercises

Between May and June 2006, after a two-day preparative workshop, the monitoring team visited 53 project sites and interviewed local stakeholders, of which 60 were contractors, 102 end users and 6 NGO representatives.[6] The WB stated several challenges at the outset of the monitoring: The Nigerian Government had handed out an incomplete list of projects that were to be funded by the Abacha funds; it had not put in place a budget system that would allow to track budget spending of the recovered Abacha assets for the monitored projects;[7] and in 2004, ongoing or already completed projects had been funded with the Abacha money in anticipation of their recovery. Namely, the Nigerian

5 Memorandum of Understanding of July 21, 2005, Agreement of September 1, 2005. For a detailed chronology see also http://www.assetrecovery.org/kc/resources/org.apache.wicket.Application/repo?nid=78488349-a33e-11dc-bf1b-335d0754ba85.

6 The following is based on oral, email as well as the WB Nigeria Public Expenditure Management and Financial Accountability Review (PEMFAR) and the NGO Shadow reports published in December 2006. The complete WB report with appendices can be downloaded at http://go.worldbank.org/NOVXDCTX40, http://go.worldbank.org/ZR3UOOP030, http://go.worldbank.org/X37TIVUGV0, http://go.worldbank.org/L9RGILS6A0, and http://go.worldbank.org/W7WW0QWYB0. The NGO Shadow Report can be accessed at http://www.aktionfinanzplatz.ch/potentatengelder.html#Nigeria_Abacha.

7 The Virtual Poverty Fund implemented in 2006 resolved this problem. It includes a budget coding system of specific projects and was created to account for the disbursement of debt relief gains under the Paris Club.

government informed the monitors that contractor arrears for the completed projects were paid; however, contractor contacts were not made available and this information could, therefore, not be confirmed. Stakeholder consultation prior to project definition was not institutionalised and poor. Furthermore, there was virtually no public communication of the funding of the projects with the recovered Abacha funds.

Apart from these challenges, a suggested policy change was clearly visible in the WB report. It recommends Nigeria's new transparency policy as follows:

Where the product of self-disclosure systematically matches the product of such independent scrutiny, there is said to be transparency. For government to be transparent therefore it has to be tolerant of public scrutiny around the information it discloses. Where stakeholders are eager to understand the 'tasks' of government, the 'processes' through which government implements the tasks, and the 'outcomes' one should expect from government activity, they could be said to be acting as 'watchdogs', particularly if the intent for gaining such knowledge is in order to hold government accountable. This forms the basis for the legitimate interest of various stakeholders, inclusive of CSOs, in the returned Abacha loot, in how it was utilized and on what outcomes are to be expected from such expenditure. 'Good' governance as previously defined in this report and as suggested by the directive principles of state policy in the Nigerian Constitution supports such levels of 'participation' from the people in their government.[8]

While the degree in which Nigeria would adopt such transparency policy recommendations in the long-term remained open, progress in this direction was stated. It is worth noting that the groundbreaking and exemplary progress was that Nigeria accepted the NGO participation in the monitoring. Moreover, Nigeria disclosed a letter to the Swiss Embassy that explained the domestic borrowing of 2004 and the detailed utilisation of the Abacha funds.

The on-site monitoring results as reported by the WB confirmed either expectation, namely proper utilisation of the funds or question-

8 WB report, p. 14.

able levels of implementation as well as evidence for over-pricing and kick-back payments known as a typical form of embezzlement in public procurement.[9]

XVIII. Comparison of the WB and the NGO shadow report

Whereas the two reports largely coincided about the quantitative findings, the Shadow Report stated several factors of implementation that concern qualitative questions regarding construction standards, community benefit of the project, etc. Specifically, it assessed both projects still in construction and completed projects under the criteria, if their degree of completion were reasonable in terms of project duration and disbursements and if, once completed, they were functional and properly equipped and staffed. It did so by virtue of detailed narratives and assessment of contract sums. 29 of the surveyed 53 projects did not meet the requirements of reasonable degree of completion or sufficient operation.[10] Predominant reasons for this were delayed disbursement of contractor payments by the Federal Government of Nigeria, contractor's abandonment or poor implementation of projects, and community vandalism due to lack of compensations for rural land expropriation or damages caused by the project. Other problems with community ownership of the projects were poor management know-how within communities, poor consultation and participation standards of the government agencies in charge of the projects and lacking prior impact assessments.[11]

Concerns about the loss of a substantial fraction of the recovered assets to corruption were raised in the Swiss Parliament and in the media.[12] However, the figure of USD 200 million of the recovered

9 ibid., p. 37, 40.
10 Shadow Report, p. 24–57.
11 ibid., p. 58–61.
12 http://www.parlament.ch/F/Suche/Pages/geschaefte.aspx?gesch_id=20065238 http://www.parlament.ch/ab/frameset/f/n/4715/234002/f_n_4715_234002_234066.htm.

Abacha funds having disappeared again was never confirmed by involved authorities and is likely to be speculative.

The Abacha monitoring exercise with NSAs participation was the first of its kind. Many political obstacles had to be removed before it became possible. Its major benefits were to create public transparency and credibility of budget disbursement as well as a basis for improving the system of public spending, a most welcome and needed effect in any emerging democracy. The initiative was also acknowledged with great international interest and Swiss NGOs were contacted by UK government agencies and French NGOs for further information on the monitoring exercise. Until today, it remains the paradigm for a truly democratic transparency policy.

XIX. Conclusion: Contributions of NSAs to asset recovery

To sum up, I would like to recall the major contributions of NSAs to asset recovery. Furthermore, it seems useful to consider the interaction of strengths of NGOs with opportunities the several stakeholders of asset recovery offer. These considerations require a reasonable degree of self-criticism of NGO actors' possible weaknesses and an assessment of threats to a sustainable asset recovery that other stakeholders may cause.

NSAs have a privileged access to local networks. They are flexible to build a network and can work over a longer time and with more resources on-site than embassy staff or government agencies can, as they have multiple responsibilities. Therefore, NGOs can deliver important information services. Furthermore, they act as policy brokers between the agencies of the receiving countries and countries of origin of stolen assets. As such agencies have stated in informal feedbacks, this NGO input strengthens the position of receiving countries and supplies policy options to countries of origin during negotiations.

The most important result of the Mobutu case discussion is that 'political will' to recover assets is no given fact, but something that can be influenced by external negotiators. In case of conflicting interests that keep the country of origin from requesting asset recovery, negotiators as well as NGO facilitators need to find out the positions of various representatives at the cabinetlevel, to identify the ones that differ from the country of origin's official position, and to co-ordinate their activities with them. The NGOs will do their part to strengthen this personal support of government representatives by virtue of their ticker service[13] and of media work.

It is worth noting that shifting the political interests in favour of a request of asset recovery will always be successful only for a limited time, normally for 12 to 18 months. It is clear that opposing forces will respond to such a development, trying to reverse it. The Mobutu case was a sad example of such a window of opportunity closing.

Moreover, NGOs contribute to implementing policy alternatives by virtue of providing expertise and financing. Finally, they strengthen public credibility in domestic politics as well as the international image to the best interest of the country of origin.

XX. Stakeholder co-operation as useful nuisance

NSAs, as the other stakeholders, too, have hidden agendas. While in countries of origin the struggle of competing and small NGOs that are poorly recognised by government agencies as well as personal career and income motivations can be stated,[14] facilitating NGOs from receiving countries need media presence to build the political pressure necessary to achieve their goals. Unsurprisingly, governments and other institutions experience these properties as nuisances to various

13 see the chapter on Mobutu.

14 In the author's view, the often criticized 'audacity' of NGO representatives in the countries of origin when discussing about remunerations is based on a fundamentally flawed Northern concept of corruption. While large scale corruption, e.g., in public procurement is rightly combated, the livelihood aspect of claims for full expatriate salary payment, e.g., for monitoring work should be duly considered in context where regular salary payments may be delayed for several months and the fiscal system fails to provide sufficient public services.

degrees. However, they acknowledge some usefulness in the NGOs promoting policy alternatives in hindsight, because of their own limited capacity and mandate to do so.

Some government actor's dogmatism about sovereignty can forestall due consideration of policy alternatives in asset recovery; this holds both for countries of origin and for receiving countries. Understandably, reluctance against considering policy alternatives may be motivated by domestic politics, as the Mobutu case shows. However, this can lead to ignoring manifest and advantageous policy options.

It is a sign of statesmanship with government representatives and of professionalism with NGOs to view these challenges to their work as part of real world partnerships.

XXI. A current civil society initiative

At the WB's conference on Asset Recovery in June 2010, European NGOs launched a Charter for Sustainable Asset Recovery. It was felt that work experience on the ground and lessons learnt need to be integrated into asset recovery policies. All hitherto cases show relevant flaws and future asset recoveries urgently need further improvement. Namely, project definition prior to recovery, a standard monitoring with NSA participation, full disclosure of contractor sums and a coding system that allows for project-by-project budget tracing are some important requirements for sustainable asset recovery that will help avoiding the assets' new disappearance.

Markus E. Schulz

The role of financial institutions in anti-bribery and anti-corruption efforts

I. Challenges and opportunities for an insurance company in its anti-bribery, anti-corruption and anti-money laundering efforts

Corruption and bribery are prevalent in all sectors and are not specific to the Financial Services industry. This sector, however, is facing some unique challenges in these fields and a specific combination of them, because such companies can be exposed to these risks in a number of ways.

When zooming in on the insurance sector it becomes apparent that bribery and corruption are critical topics across the entire value chain. Insurance companies are exposed to potential bribery and corruption risks when closing new deals, when settling claims, when purchasing large goods and services contracts and of course the risk that the proceeds of bribery and corruption will be placed with an insurance company in a number of products.

As a result, this is a very important topic in the insurance industry which receives due attention from both the business and compliance functions. Many, if not all, companies have had measures, rules and controls in place for years which have been driven by local anti-bribery and anti-corruption regulations as well as extraterritorial ones such as the FCPA of the USA and more recently the Bribery Act in the UK.

While those extraterritorial regulations have not fundamentally changed the way insurance companies conduct business, they have triggered reviews, enhancements and a further globalisation of their anti-bribery and anti-corruption frameworks.

II. The corner stones of a robust anti-bribery and anti-corruption framework

Let's take a few steps back to have a look at how an insurance company addresses this topic and builds up the respective controls. This summary is an amalgamation of controls and approaches observed at a number of companies in the Insurance industry and do not describe those of one in particular.

Tone from the top – This is somewhat needless to say but an effective framework starts and stops with the management's approach to this topic. There needs to be a commitment by the executive management, as well as any supervisory board, to make this a priority across the firm. It should become part of the corporate DNA, like 'doing the right thing' generally. This term is used often and sounds good however there is no universal definition and it means different things to different people. It is therefore important to work with senior management to set the tone from the top and ensure that it becomes a part of each day's operation. Simple things such as top management making a reference in a speech or briefly talking about it at an employee gathering are quick wins that will help to set the tone and pave the way for a successful compliance framework.

With the right tone from the top established, the compliance function can build the appropriate anti-bribery and anti-corruption framework and design the controls together with the business to ensure that the policy and standards agreed with the board will be implemented in all areas of the company and will become operational.

The best compliance controls are those that are not compliance controls!

This sounds like a paradox at first and appears to speak against the compliance function however it simply means that the appropriate controls for the business to conduct their activities in a compliant way are so well embedded in the day-to-day operations, that they become business as usual, so that the business is automatically compliant when executing their normal business processes. At first glance this appears to be a very simple and obvious approach but in practice, this is far too often not the case and often compliance controls are 'bolted' onto the business processes, maybe even as separate stand-alone processes, creating the feeling within the business that there are extra 'compliance' steps to conduct. By baking compliance controls into the business processes they shall become invisible to the business and the feeling of an extra 'compliance burden' should reduce and may even vanish.

This embedding of controls requires a close co-operation between compliance and the business. It is not about taking over the business responsibilities in this process, but is about advising them on how to design controls, how to operate and oversee them best and how to establish a sound follow-up procedure. To be able to do this and to be a partner for the business the respective compliance personnel must have a good understanding of the business and their processes and the general operational environment. This should motivate the recruitment of more 'business people' into the compliance function in order to establish an effective balance of skills and experience within the compliance teams.

In general, compliance controls, no matter where they are established or executed within the firm, should adhere to a 'less is often more' principle. This is particularly the case if those selective and targeted controls get executed well, with proper and regular oversight, reporting and follow-up. This is preferable to establishing many controls which are then executed with minimal attention and no follow-up. It's about the quality of controls not about the quantity: many controls do not automatically mean a company is in control.

From the tone at the top a group-wide framework and approach should be developed and established. For a multi-national company it appears to be beneficial to have a consistent approach across the franchise to protect the name and the brand. If, for example, facilitation payments are prohibited in one part of the company, but it is common practice in another, this will make it difficult for the business to operate; it will raise questions with regulators and even customers and partners that may touch the company in multiple parts of the business and geographies.

Such a group-wide framework should have a solid foundation and multiple pillars to support a strong structure and the tone from the top.

The foundation is formed by an anti-bribery and anti-corruption group policy to set the standard for the corporation and to guide all subsequent efforts. It should be a translation of the (often multiple) external requirements into simple (business) language and should not be a copy of the external legal texts and regulations. Such a document should be designed and written for the business and not for lawyers. The starting point for external requirements will always be local legal and regulatory obligations and expectations. It is important to also capture any recent developments and expectations that have been voiced by supervisors, which often indicate future enhancements and alterations of regulations and will help the internal company policy to be more future-proof and more positively received when reviewed by regulators. After this, extraterritorial requirements need to be assessed and validated to what extend they may apply to the business model and operations of the company. For many companies that meant the FCPA in the past, but now also includes the UK Bribery Act. The UK Bribery Act is a relatively new requirement and while the Act had been signed in April 2010 it took many months for the final guidance to come out in March 2011. Given that it has been a relatively new regulation at the time of publication of this paper, there is only a certain level of interpretation and guidance available to provide companies clarity on the extent they should or must apply this Bribery Act to their global operations. What we see in the industry though is that most companies do consider the requirements of the UK Bribery Act regardless of whether it directly impacts those companies or not. It is perceived good practice to consider both the UK Bribery Act and the FCPA of the US, when determining extraterritorial requirements. Other countries may follow in future and so it is important to design a policy and framework that is flexible enough with an open architecture to respond quickly to such changes.

Many other aspects of a holistic compliance programme will build on this foundation to create the framework a global corporation requires these days. Every new policy will need communication, awareness and training. It may require dedicated officers in local units to look after the topic. Those may be organised in a global network to efficiently and effectively manage the theme across the firm. It may require some systems to automate certain controls. It will require some level of testing and monitoring. To what extent those efforts will be required all depend on the size of the company, its geographical spread, its product mix and its business-operating model. A separate chapter could be written solely about those, but this is not necessarily specific to anti-bribery and anti-corruption or AML, but more generically applies to all compliance topics and will not be expanded on here.

III. The dimensions of bribery and corruption risks within an insurance company

All those activities will establish a strong framework and puts the company in a good starting position. But, what's next?

Some business areas are naturally more exposed than others in an insurance company, like it is the case for other industries as well, and consequently they should receive some more attention than other areas and units and may carry different controls.

The insurance market is a very competitive environment and a number of insurance companies are competing for the big and interesting deals. Generally speaking the compliance risks are different in personal lines than corporate business, with personal line insurance being the business with consumers. The personal lines business is a high volume insurance business with moderate insurance values and low premium sums. In the corporate insurance business the dynamics are different with the contract values being high and the volume of customers relatively low. Naturally there are a number of sub-segments within the corporate business from the bakery around the corner to a Fortune 500 company and anything in between. As a result not all pose the same potential risk with regards to bribery and corruption.

In the mid and large corporate segment the business usually gets placed through an insurance broker and the broker works on behalf of the customer, unlike an insurance agent who works on behalf of the insurer. Those brokers are supposed to offer the whole of the market to the insurance seeker and shall offer the products best suited to the needs of the entity looking for insurance cover.

With the broker representing the client the broker is also the party in between the prospect and the insurance company. Due to the set-up of that relationship, there could be a temptation to influence a broker by offering benefits that the broker would receive from one insurance company but not another. This could range from 'gestures' offered to the broker during the actual sales and underwriting process in order to win this particular deal, to building up general goodwill with a broker to increase the chance that the broker will approach a specific insurer first or allow an insurer to quote exclusively initially, or to influence the broker which insurance products they will offer to the insurance seeking prospect.

Over the past years there have been numerous instances published in the press or by regulators where insurance companies have been found to inappropriately influence a broker.

Many may picture envelopes being exchanged or other such obvious bribes, but there are more subtle ways that the relationship could be exploited. Examples include inviting brokers to lavish entertainment or events, sponsoring brokers to the attendance of a high profile industry event, inviting them to an insurance training or product presentation in an exotic location for a week where the actual presentation of the product lasts two hours, etc. Such bribery and corruption can take very creative forms and will evolve and change over time.

Controls are key, no doubt, but more important are the culture of a company and the business conduct of each employee, as controls are limited in their range and effectiveness and a compliance function cannot monitor each and every business transaction, customer interaction or business event. It needs to be in the DNA of the company and each employee to distinguish appropriate from inappropriate behaviour. Compliance is the second line of defence and the business is the first one. At the same time it is not suggested to put all reliance on the corporate DNA and risk-based checks and balances are required without any doubt. Those checks and balances are not only to tick the regulatory box but are in the interest of the business and the long-term success of the company helping to win and maintain sustainable and profitable business.

All companies are under similar pressures to win new business and this could bear the risk that a sales person may take a short cut or try to win business in an inappropriate way or simply overlooks certain control steps when work load and pressure mount.

Governments often utilize a tender process and put Requests for Proposals (RFPs) in the market for multiple insurance companies to bid for the business. In those situations the risk for an insurer increases if the sales people are close with the person or team who runs the RFP process to try and obtain additional information the competition may not have access to or to influence the decision making. An obvious one would be to treat those decision makers differently to other clients and provide them with disproportionate and extraordinary benefits or treats. The less obvious is the influencing of these processes through third parties.

There were some recent prominent cases that were reported in the international press where insurance companies and brokers had allegedly made payments to agents, lawyers and consultants who supported the process of winning the business. In some countries local agencies may be required to be able to get the necessary support in the local language or a consultant to advice on how to conduct business appropriately in a foreign country or a law firm to help the contract negotiations, where the company may have no presence or never did business before. These services are legitimate and are regularly being used and not only by insurance companies in order to better navigate through the 'jungle of globalisation'. The problem starts when those agents receive payments disproportionate to the services they offer and the work they carry out. As we learned from various cases that have been publicised, agents and third parties have redirected some of the payments they received to bribe (foreign) officials to influence the outcome of such RFPs or deals.

Those third parties act independently of the insurer, but of course support the insurer's interest in winning the business. As non-employees they are more difficult to control and so the entire process of dealing with third parties in the context of winning new business requires dedicated controls and enhanced monitoring. Amongst others the risk increases by the extra layer that third parties add to the process and the limited control over these independent parties.

There are other areas of increased risk in the insurance sector that may differ from some other sectors in the financial services industry.

In general the generation of new business is an area of friction for bribery and corruption for companies in the financial services industry and beyond. In insurance there is another significant area of bribery risk, which is the handling of claims.

It is the nature of an insurance contract that it may pay out as a result of a risk event occurring and the subsequent settling of the claim. The risk event can be anything from a car accident to a fire in a factory, or an earthquake to the liability of a company director.

In this case the focus is not so much on the insurer giving bribes to obtain a business benefit, but to protect the insurer from being bribed by a claimant to obtain a benefit.

Some claims are straightforward, clear and don't leave much room for interpretation from either the insurer or the claimant. There are other more complex cases where it often is a very difficult and tedious process to establish the exact sum due for the claimant or even establishing the fact of whether the event or sum claimed is covered by the terms of the insurance policy. In those cases the insurance company is at risk that a claimant may try to influence the claims adjuster through inappropriate behaviour or benefits. The coffee that a claim adjuster is being offered when inspecting a wreckage car on-site is less of a concern and it is not the intention to stop any general friendly behaviour; however, there need to be clear rules and standards to ensure that friendly behaviour does not turn into a bribe. Examples can include arranging the inspection of that wreckage car in the evening and then inviting the claims adjuster for dinner maybe with some expensive wine or in an expensive restaurant, or in a case where the claims handler is dealing with a complex industry claim and is being offered to shop at preferential employee prices in the factory store that would not be available to ordinary people, or the invitation to a corporate event and so on. In those cases the risk is increased that this gesture may influence the objectivity of the claims handler and could lead to an unjustified benefit for the claimant and a loss for the insurer.

Many claims departments have, as a result, opted for a zero tolerance gifts policy and do not permit their claims people to accept anything from a company, claimant or broker who looks after the insured's interests. This goes as far as the claim adjuster paying their share of a business dinner, if the dinner was the only opportunity to discuss the claim situation with the claimant and the claims adjuster then needing to refuse the vintage bottle of wine that was ordered.

Then there is the third dimension where an insurance company is exposed to bribery and corruption risk. This is a dimension which is no different to any other corporation and applies to the private as well as the public sector. This is the procurement process of a company.

An insurance company is special in that there are two major procurement areas. The first one is the procuring of goods and services to run the operation of a company including office supplies, furniture, software or consultancy services. This is the area not specific to insurance. Noticeably, times have changed and procurement officers are less likely to be invited to the paid-for product demonstration or user group on the owner's yacht in Monaco or the Caribbean these days. Despite those different times, regulation and general perception on such benefits companies who want to sell their goods and services remain creative and constantly invent new ways to dine, entertain and treat customers and prospects.

The procurement area more specific to the insurance industry is the procurement as part of the claims handling and settlement. Many insurance companies have moved away from settling all claims in cash and utilize their significant purchasing power to purchase replacements or repair services for their claimants to handle the insured event. In those cases vendors race for preferred supplier status knowing that this will bring a steady flow of business and income, although it may require a discounted price of the service given the competition, but it still is very attractive to companies and gives them access to new prospects.

Controls will be required in both areas of procurement to ensure that the company gets the best deal and not the deal that was best for the person handling the purchase on behalf of the company.

IV. Understanding the relative risks to enable a true risk-based approach

So in summary, there are three dimensions where an insurance company faces most risk for bribery and corruption:

- New business
- Claims handling
- Procurement

The procurement area is the same for all corporations and as such all companies will have the same interests. It is more delicate to strike the right balance and level of controls for new business and claims handling to not become less competitive.

Needless to say, being most competitive should not be the driver for designing the anti-bribery and anti-corruption controls and policy of an insurance company. However, the company needs to remain competitive and not drown in controls and additional process steps that unnecessarily increase the costs of doing business with the result of needing to be more expensive and thus less attractive than the competition.

A risk-based approach is the answer. Having adequate and targeted controls rather than 'one size fits all'.

But what does this actually mean? Many people have different definitions and views on this and it is also an area of unease for some, as it means there are no prescriptive rules that one can look at, implement and tick the box. It requires analytical skills and needs judgement. This, however, is the only way to get maximum control instilled in an organization while at the same time limiting impact on its operation, processes and ultimately cost base.

To benefit from a risk-based approach a company needs to understand the risks inherent in its operation. It also means that it needs to have a solid understanding where these risks are and what relative potential risk they pose. It is a must to have a robust risk assessment process in place that will help to identify any inherent potential risks initially and maintain that view on a regular basis. At least once a year this should be repeated to ensure the controls are still adequate and not too less or too much due a number of variables such as business practices changing, the introduction of new systems, a shift in the customer base, the product mix or the like. In addition, a focused risk assessment should be embedded in the product development process to ensure new products do not introduce unidentified risks and therefore unmanaged risks.

As a side note, a risk assessment should never be conducted by an assurance function in isolation and instead offers an opportunity to engage with the business and to raise awareness in the business on the topic, the inherent risks and the mitigating controls that will be required as a result of the risk assessment. Too often the risk assessment is conducted without the involvement of the business and only the result is presented back to the business, which quickly results in discussions about the outcome and diverts the energy away from mitigating identified risks. Besides, it is an opportunity for the assurance function to refresh their business knowledge and also to do some 'marketing' for the function, as face-time with the business sometimes is difficult to arrange given the pressures the business is under and all their priorities.

The outcome of the risk assessment will enable the company to establish targeted and focused controls in the area needed and will spare processes that have proven to have no inherent risks. This is a win-win situation saving costs and preserving the competitiveness, both of which the business will support.

In the end however, there still may be the argument 'but no one else is having these controls' or 'our competitors do this, why can't we' or most often heard 'this is market practice, so why should we not do/stop it?' At this stage it will be vital to have the right tonc from the top as mentioned earlier on and a supportive corporate DNA. Equally though it is all too easy to hide behind a board decision using the line 'sorry, this has been decided by the board, we must …'. Unfortunately, sometimes little time is spent on explaining the 'WHY'. Why are we doing certain things and why are we not supporting others? That's what the business and others affected want to understand. And it is not just the business; it's human nature that we want to know the 'why' behind something. It has proven to be so much easier to establish controls if one understands the why, which will create acceptance and buy-in making an opponent a supporter of the proposed process.

This will require some time initially, but will pay back in the mid-term and will create a more sustainable environment and also add to the strengthening of the corporate DNA.

V. Bribes need to be laundered to appear legitimate

And finally there is a fourth dimension where an insurance company is exposed to bribery and corruption risks. This very much depends on the product range offered by an insurer and mainly affects the Life insurance products. In particular the asset accumulating type of products within the Life and Pension product range are exposed to be (mis)used by corrupt people to hide and disguise bribes they have received.

For very good reasons AML rules apply to the life insurance sector as well, to ensure that controls are adequate in order to keep illicit funds out of the system, such as bribes and the proceed from corruption. Not all products of a life insurer pose the same risk though. For example, a term life insurance policy covers the life of an individual and does not have a savings component to it, meaning it will only pay in case of death and only the assured sum and does not pay out any paid-in premiums. This situation changes in a life insurance product that has a savings component embedded in it and builds up a cash value over the policy's lifetime. Those life insurance policies may or may not have a significant death cover on top of the investment funds paid in.

The differentiating factor is that there will be no funds paid out in case a term life insurance policy is cancelled, as the premium was solely to cover the insured risk, which did not occur. For investment type life insurance the funds will be paid out in case a product with a savings component is cancelled and which has accumulated a cash value. For those products the premium has two components: one is the risk premium (same as for the term assurance) and the other element, usually the much bigger part of the premium, is the savings component that results in the accumulation of a cash value during the duration of those insurance policies. Where to apply what level of controls will be determined through a risk assessment to enable the risk-based approach as mentioned beforehand.

It is vital for any life insurance company to clearly establish the source of wealth for customers when they want to invest in a life insurance policy. This is similar to banking and with a comparable level of due diligence. Important to mention in this context is the risk-based approach once more, at the risk of sounding repetitive. Even in investment type life insurance policies that accumulate a cash value the same due diligence need not be applied to all levels, i.e. not to all policy values. The 3rd European Union Directive on Money Laundering even supports that low value life insurance contracts with monthly premium payments not in excess of EUR 1.000 per annum or a lump sum premium of EUR 2.500 qualify for simplified due diligence and do not require the same processes as higher value policies. Within the simplified due diligence regime it is not required to establish the source of wealth, given the low risk of money laundering. It would be disproportionate to apply the same due diligence process for a life insurance policy that has a monthly premium of EUR 50 and one that has a lump sum initial investment of EUR 250.000. As a general rule it can be applied that the higher the premium the more due diligence steps are required and depending on the jurisdiction, different mandatory documentation must be obtained in addition to the documentation and evidence that the insurance company may require.

Every bribery and corruption event will trigger a subsequent money laundering event, as the beneficiary of those illicit funds needs to integrate it in the system and must try to make them appear legitimate funds. If those funds cannot be used for the interests of the beneficiary, then it is less of an interest for that person to accept the bribe in first place. They want to use those illicit and criminal proceeds to enhance their lifestyle, to pay back debt or to spend it on luxury items. This all can only be done safely and easily if the funds have been integrated in the system and since banks have put up high barriers for laundering assets after years of investments in strong AML controls, regulation and regulatory scrutiny, launderers look for alternative ways and methods. Industries with large value cash flows lend themselves to being an attractive alternative to the traditional banking channel and some insurance products fit that bill. Over recent years statistics and experience indicate that the insurance industry is more exposed today with more laundering attempts being detected and prevented then it ever was and regulatory interest has followed suit.

Insurance companies are very aware of this and one of the areas that was identified as an increased risk area are PEPs, especially those that have decision power over significant governmental budgets or who are influential in the decision-making process. An example would be the state head of the military and the defence budget where a decision is due to make a significant purchase of new military equipment. The sums involved are usually very high and so are the stakes for the bidding companies.

It is therefore important to identify PEPs during the on-boarding process, so that those customers can be put through the enhanced due diligence process and later on be subject to enhanced on-going monitoring. To avoid any doubt or misinterpretation, this shall not imply that every PEP is corrupt or criminal; it merely reflects their exposed status and the heightened risk that they may pose. Most AML regulations have identified PEPs as an increased risk category and require specific and dedicated processes for those, following the FATF recommendation (no. 6). Identifying PEPs during the on-boarding is not sufficient though, as a person could purchase a life insurance contract before moving into politics and while he was not a PEP during the on-boarding, the customer may become one during the lifetime of the insurance policy and should the political level be senior enough this will add a level of risk.

The complexity grows further if (shell) companies, trusts, foundations and other structures are utilized for the investment of illicit funds and bribes, adding a layer of complexity to establish transparency to identify beneficial ownership and potential PEPs or one of their associated parties that may be behind such a company or who may control it.

This all sounds great in theory and is the right approach. It is unfortunately much more complicated and complex when it comes to implementing and operating such a process in the daily business activities and on-going application.

Who is a Politically Exposed Person? When do they become one? Is a Mayor of a mountain village with 100 inhabitants as exposed as the mayor of New York? Is a low ranking politician early on in their career as exposed as the head of state?

There are many definitions of a PEP and this makes the application no easier. In addition, where does one source the information from, where does an institution get this list from to put their reliance on? Unlike for trade and economic sanctions, there are no official PEP lists maintained by the United Nation or any other supra national body nor any government. So it is down to the private sector to make this work and for companies to choose an appropriate definition for their AML policy and to source the data from a private sector vendor. Those so-called list aggregators have specialised their research activities to identify political hierarchies in a country and to pull all this information together in one database (list) for the industry to purchase. There are a number of vendors out there and as a result multiple versions of a global PEP list. On the top levels they are comparable, as it is obvious that the head of States and their direct ministers are politically exposed, but the further down it goes in the political organization of a country the more difficult it gets and this is where the proprietary definitions of the list aggregators start to differ.

If this would not be complicated enough already it is amplified by the fact that it is not only the PEPs an institution needs to identify, but also their spouses, other family members and close associates. This is the area where the definitions and the lists differ more significantly, as it comes down to the list aggregator's proprietary research.

For years the industry is asking for a publicly available list. The argument made by regulators and lawmakers was that this is too complicated to obtain and manage. Exactly that is the challenge for the private sector, too, but why is it that each institution needs to re-invent the wheel and the effort could not be made once and shared across the industry. This is not perceived as an area of Anti-Competition and only if the industry works closely together and with the regulatory authorities can we jointly be successful in the global anti-bribery, anti-corruption and anti-money laundering efforts.

Looking at this apparently impossible task to create governmental driven PEP lists it may be less complex and more possible when approaching it in a certain way. Agreed, to provide one consolidated list may be too complicated and something for the future, but smaller steps closer to home may get us further than is the general belief. Who knows better their PEPs than a country itself? So if each country would publish a list of who they consider a PEP in their country this would get the industry a long way and will lay the foundation of an eventual global list. Perhaps not aggregated in one format or source, which is of lesser concern to the industry initially and it is very likely that there will be vendors who would facilitate this job like they do for the trade and economic sanctions lists already. It should be noted that these trade and economic sanctions lists are published by governments today. Ideally all states would agree on one format to make the handling of the lists easier, but even in the absence of a uniform format, governmental published lists would take away much of today's ambiguity.

Maybe this is something the FATF could add to their agenda for the coming years. Sometimes the argument is made that this would have data privacy concerns. That point however is difficult to maintain as a PEP is by its very nature exposed to the public and most likely has much information in the public domain already and the information required for a PEP list are not many elements next to name of the PEP and their function.

Financial institutions are limited to what they can do on background checks and do not have unlimited resources to do an enhanced due diligence on all customers. Celent has published a report in July 2011 that has put the total costs for AML programs across financial institutions at a staggering USD 5.8 billion. These are the total costs of all AML controls, technology and people operating those controls, AML assessments and investigations. They also estimated the annual costs growth at around 10% year on year. All those costs will need to be funded and consequently find their way into the pricing of the financial services products ultimately.

By looking across the various regulations discussed in this chapter it appears obvious that there are synergies and opportunities for the anti-money laundering and anti-bribery and anti-corruption regulations and regulators to work together more closely, particularly in the area of Politically Exposed Persons and due diligence. Bribes end in laundered money and this connection does not yet flow through regulations the same way.

ANNE LUGON-MOULIN

The role of donors in supporting NSAs in the asset recovery process

I. Introduction

Development assistance agencies have worked with NSAs for many decades and in a variety of sectors.[1] NSAs are thus extremely important players in a number of development assistance types of intervention: in prevention and awareness-raising efforts in specific policy issues (e.g., human rights, access to information), in supplementing or replacing governmental functions when those have almost or totally collapsed (e.g., health services, education services in post-crisis contexts), in monitoring government actions (e.g., state budget monitoring, corruption monitoring), or in implementing projects upon mandate of donors' agencies, as a majority of donors projects, if not dedicated to financing governmental structures, are implemented via civil society organisations.

As starting point, it might be useful to circumscribe the subject of asset recovery in the donor intervention landscape. Asset recovery is a sub-topic under the anti-corruption agenda, which comprises a range of activities, from legal reforms to advocacy. And anti-corruption itself is a sub-topic in the governance sector. This article will focus exclusively on the role of donors in working with NSAs in the asset recovery process. It will not discuss how to work with NSAs in broader anti-corruption or governance programmes, although it is

This chapter was submitted by Ms. Lugon-Moulin in her individual capacity, and does not necessarily reflect the views of the Swiss Agency for Development and Co-operation.

1 In the development cooperation jargon, 'civil society organization' or 'civil society' are the terms used for meaning 'non state actor'.

sometimes difficult to disentangle those as they have clear linkages and synergies.[2]

Before describing and analysing the various avenues of collaboration between donors and NSAs, this paper will recall how and when the asset recovery agenda appears on the development assistance screen. Thereafter, four main avenues of collaboration will be described in light of concrete examples: capacity building of asset recovery actors, payment of lawyers' fees, advocacy work and investigation, as well as mechanisms for repatriating of stolen assets. Taking into account some lessons learnt, some concluding remarks will sketch out the future of NSAs work and donors interventions in asset recovery.

II. History

A rapid historical overview might be helpful to understand where donors stand with regard to the asset recovery agenda. This topic, which was previously exclusively the work of law enforcement authorities, came to the limelight of the international community at the time of the UNCAC negotiations in the early 2000s. Contrary to the other and older anti-corruption conventions (the OECD Anti-Bribery Convention; the Civil and Criminal Law Conventions against Corruption of the CoE), which address bribery and other specific corruption forms, the UNCAC encompasses a wider range of governance issues, such as public finances or public procurement, which can potentially be subject of corruption or embezzlement. After a long process of negotiations where the numerous participating countries had to find common grounds in their sometimes conflicting national interests, asset recovery became finally part of the convention (chapter V).[3] The

2 See Lugon-Moulin Anne, in 'Les traités internationaux contre la corruption', ed. Balmelli, T., and Jaggy, B., 2004, for a detailed analysis on the work with civil society.

3 See Jaggy B., in 'Les traités internationaux contre la corruption' , ed. Balmelli, T., and Jaggy, B., for a detailed description of the negotiation process of the UNCAC.

UNCAC is the first attempt to acknowledge stolen assets as an issue to be tackled internationally.

This convention also contains a chapter on technical assistance (chapter VI), pointing at the needs to help developing and transition countries in their battle against corruption in all issues covered in the remaining chapters, and therefore specifically targeting the donor agencies. This is how the development co-operation agencies became aware of the asset recovery problem, as being part of the corruption problematic. They realised that the recovery of the proceeds of corruption was actually the end of a long chain of factors: this chain starts from the state of extremely bad governance framework in certain developing countries where impunity and the lack of internal and external control mechanisms allow PEPs to easily steal assets from the national budget, and ends with the co-operation between law enforcement authorities of both the requesting and the requested states in order to recover those stolen assets deposited in financial centres. Until then, donors were traditionally devoted to tackling the governance framework in the recipient countries, namely the beginning of the chain, by funding programmes aiming at, for instance, improving the legal framework of a country, strengthening its justice sector or its public finances management system. But donors were not used to provide assistance to tackle specific corruption cases, which were considered as a pure domestic matter left to the concerned law enforcement authorities. This is the major novelty in asset recovery, as a development and anti-corruption topic.

Another political debate led to having asset recovery put on the international agenda, and specifically on the donors' agenda. Along with the international wave of criticism towards development assistance which emerged at the end of the last decade,[4] international development agencies have been increasingly put under pressure, and have been asked to demonstrate the usefulness and the appropriateness of their mandate.

4 This wave of criticism – which is still on-going – coincides with a landmark, namely the 50 years of independence of former colonies. At this point, donors are required to prove the effectiveness of their actions.

The ODA budget in 2010, which has been recently released by the OECD, amounts to USD 129 billion. The WB estimates that the total global cross-border flow of proceeds from criminal activities, corruption and tax evasion may reach USD 1.6 trillion per year, nearly half of which comes from developing nations. A recent study from GFI also found that losses from illicit flows from developing countries are estimated between USD 858.6 billion and USD 1.06 trillion annually. Although the accuracy of this figure can be questioned, as money outflows coming from various malpractices are taken into consideration.[5] When the ODA figure and the corruption figures are compared, one necessarily comes to the conclusion that the risk of development assistance vanishing in corruption flows is very high. This is an additional reason why donors have a duty to *tackle stolen assets from* the onset. Countries having a vivid financial centre, likely to accept part of those illegally acquired assets by PEPs from developing and transition countries, have been put under pressure to act also in their domestic environment, in order to prevent further looting worldwide and ensuring to move away from a dual morality system, whereby good governance principles are preached abroad and loose practices can be tolerated domestically. This necessity is now reflected as an important so-called 'policy coherence' issue, which has recently appeared prominently in the OECD Development Assistance Committee's agenda. Policy coherence is one of the criteria for evaluating industrialised countries' aid system.[6]

Switzerland has a long track record in asset recovery cases. Down through those cases, several solutions have been applied, where NSAs and donors have been directly associated. This paper will therefore primarily discuss the various roles of NSAs in the asset recovery process based on the experience of Switzerland as a requested state in the asset recovery process and also as a donor. It will also illustrate other international efforts.

5 http://www.unodc.org/pdf/Star_FactSheet.pdf.

6 See OECD, Examen du CAD par les Pairs : Suisse, 2009.

III. Capacity building of requesting states' law enforcement bodies

In 2003, Switzerland's law enforcement authorities had to deal with the case of a former prime Minister of an African country. In 2007, after a long judicial process, the frozen proceeds of crime unfortunately had to be returned to the owner, due to failure of the requestingd state authorities to sufficiently prove the illicit origin of the funds. After the closure of the case, and in collaboration with the Swiss law enforcement authorities, SDC offered to send a Swiss federal prosecutor to help the authorities in understanding the Swiss legal requirements in a MLA procedure, and in investigating future cases. This effort proved to be useful, but was a one-off action. For obvious reasons, it is difficult for full-time prosecutors working in Switzerland to take days off to be sent abroad in order to help their counterparts in developing or transition countries.

A systematic technical assistance would require a long-term organised structure, composed of full-time staff. In 2006, SDC started to set up the ICAR, based at the Basel Institute on Governance, a Swiss Foundation. The ICAR has the mandate to assist public officials and law enforcement authorities in developing and transition countries in anti-corruption cases investigation, mutual legal assistance request drafting and handling, and asset recovery procedures, for example by providing strategic advice on specific cases or with customized training programs. The Principality of Liechtenstein and the DfID have been taken on board as additional core donors of the ICAR shortly after its creation. To date, other bilateral agencies and multilateral agencies fund a wide range of activities of the ICAR. As a civil society organisation, or so-called NSA, the ICAR offers various advantages. Firstly, by employing experienced prosecutors and investigators, the ICAR is able to respond flexibly and quickly to capacity building demands worldwide and works on a long-term basis with law enforcement authorities of various countries. Secondly, it works on behalf of several countries and therefore doesn't formally represent anybody's particular interests. It is perfectly positioned to act as a facilitator.

However, the work of the ICAR also has limitations when working on specific cases. The organisation has no status of an international organisation and cannot undertake the full-fledged work of a lawyer, represent formally a country's interests, or undertake litigation. One can also claim that by assisting one party only (usually the developing/transition country who lacks sufficient knowledge and skills), ICAR may not be seen as completely neutral. The immense added value of ICAR is therefore its general long-term capacity building programmes in various countries.

IV. Payment of private law firms fees

In order to help requesting states in interacting with Swiss authorities for concrete cases (compliance with MLA requirements, asset recovery investigations and litigation) and to accelerate procedures, Switzerland has come up with an innovative solution in the past which is faster than capacity building. The country paid lawyers to represent the requesting state's interests throughout Swiss proceedings. Private law firms have proved to be very helpful in providing direct knowledge of the Swiss legal and judicial system and in tracing and recovering assets abroad. In 1993 already, in agreement with the FDJ, the SDC has begun financing such an arrangement in the case of Moussa Traoré, former dictator in Mali. In 1991, Mali requested MLA for confiscating the illegally acquired assets deposited in Switzerland. The procedure ended successfully in 1997 with CHF 3.9 million finally repatriated to the democratic government of President Konaré.[7] The payment of lawyer's fees became again relevant a decade later with the Abacha case. The Swiss government again offered the Nigerian authorities the services of a private law firm based in Geneva in order to accelerate procedures between both states. In this example, the funding did not come from SDC, but from the FDJ itself. The dif-

7 Lugon-Moulin A., 'Asset Recovery: concrete challenges for development assistance', in Pieth, M. (ed). *Recovering Stolen Assets*, 2008, p. 302.

ficulties encountered in the more recent cases of Duvalier (Haïti) and Mobutu (DRC) again raised the question of helping those requesting states which were unable to fulfil the requirements of the Swiss judicial authorities. In both cases, reliable evidence was needed from the requesting state as answers to legal assistance provided by Switzerland. However, both judicial systems were so deficient that those countries were unable to conduct criminal proceedings in such a way as to comply with the minimal requirements of a correct judicial procedure respecting the rule of law. As a result of this, legal assistance had to stop after several attempts.[8] The same unfortunate outcome arises if the requesting State does not press charges against the PEP, or if the criminal proceedings are not followed up after having been initiated: the Swiss authorities have no choice but to close the case and unfreeze the assets.

In order to avoid such an outcome, a Swiss lawyer, again financed by the SDC, was hired to assist the Haitian government in the Duvalier case. The same offer was presented to the Congolese government in the same period. For the former case, after a long process and several hiccups, and the entering into force of the new RIAA, the prospects are good that the monies will eventually be returned to the people of Haiti. However, in the latter case, the Congolese authorities have never given a formal answer to the Swiss proposal and the Congolese judicial authorities have not followed up the proceedings. The CHF 3 million frozen in Swiss accounts had thus to be returned to the Mobutu family. Those unfortunate developments in the late 2000s paved the ground for issuing this new asset recovery law (RIAA), which specifically tackles the problems of having to deal with weak law enforcement authorities in so-called 'fragile states', such as Haiti or DRC at the moment of their requests.[9]

8 Morier P.-Y., 'Is autonomous confiscation the acme of asset recovery ?', in Pieth, M. (ed). *Recovering Stolen Assets*, 2008, p. 274.

9 The new Restitution of Illicit Assets Act (RIAA) aims to : establish a formal legal basis for the practice of the Federal Council when it comes to the freezing of assets so that, when the process of international mutual legal assistance fails to produce the desired results, it will no longer have to be based on Art. 184, Para. 3, of the Federal Constitution; avoid having to undertake the restitution of illicit assets to politically exposed persons (PEPs) because of the failure of state

The fact that the development agency of a requested state has funded a few asset recovery efforts, by way of paying private law firms' services acting on behalf of the requesting state, is quite unique. Such solutions demonstrate a strong willingness from specific individuals within the state apparatus to seek pragmatic solutions in order to solve cases aiming at the best outcome for the requesting and the requested countries. For doing so, Swiss judicial authorities have not refrained from getting in contact with the Ministry of Foreign Affairs, an executive body, slightly pushing the boundaries of the separation of powers. To our knowledge, very few countries have replicated this type of solution. The DfID funded the legal proceedings in British civil courts with a grant of USD 2 million in the case of Chiluba, former president of Zambia.[10] The Netherlands submitted a proposal at the CoSP of the UNCAC in 2006 for creating a multi-donor Trust Fund, which would serve the purpose of financing the necessary law firm expertise for specific asset recovery cases worldwide.[11] After a long and vivid debate, the CoSP in the end did not adopt this ambitious proposal for a number of reasons, among which national political considerations, conflicting interests, practical technicalities as well as developmental doubts certainly played a role. The matter was again taken up at the CoSP in Bali in 2008, but in the meantime, it has lost momentum and has not appeared high on the agenda. At the Doha CoSP in 2009, it was almost not an issue any more.

From a development and donors' perspective, such financial arrangements are certainly very innovative in the realm of anti-corruption efforts. They open doors to working at home, with domestic actors, thereby improving policy coherence in a highly debated and

structures in the state concerned, by providing for their administrative forfeiture; provide a formal legal basis and guidelines for the restitution of assets confiscated for the benefit of the country of origin; to date Swiss law has no provision to determine such matters; the solutions adopted in the past have therefore been ad hoc. (http://www.eda.admin.ch/eda/en/home/topics/finec/intcr/poexp/faqria.0001.html#faq0001).

10 For detailed information about this complicated case judgement: http://www.bailii.org/ew/cases/EWHC/Ch/2007/952.html.

11 De Jong Cornelis, 'The role of donors', in Pieth, M. (ed). *Recovering Stolen Assets*, 2008, p. 313.

political topic. But they are considered as short-term solutions without any impact on sustainability in partner countries: by having an external actor performing the work of domestic law enforcement authorities, the requesting state does not have the space and the opportunity to build its own judicial capacity. The structural issues of weak law enforcement system, underdeveloped skills and the lack of human and financial resources within law enforcement authorities remain, even though some cross-learning effects can still happen.

V. Advocacy work and investigation

In awareness-raising and advocacy work, donors are used to working with NSAs to stimulate the debate around important topics. To date, however, international NSAs have been relatively quiet with regard to the asset recovery agenda. Tax evasion – albeit linked to asset recovery – has attracted a lot more attention. It is for example one of the key topic addressed by the Task Force on Economic Integrity and Economic Development, to date funded by NORAD and the government of Spain, and dedicated to advocating for improved transparency and accountability in the global financial system. TI, funded by many more bilateral donors (including Switzerland) more than fifteen years, has been absolutely instrumental in the emergence of the OECD Anti-Bribery Convention and the UNCAC, but the international leading anti-corruption NSA has never been at the forefront of the battle in asset recovery, tax evasion or money laundering. Somehow, this field of action seems to have been left to national NSAs. Some national TI chapters directly concerned by specific PEPs monies (TI France, TI Switzerland, some African chapters), though, have been much more vocal. For example, TI France and the French Sherpa Association have deposited a legal complaint against ruling families of Angola, Burkina Faso, Congo-Brazzaville, Equatorial Guinea and Gabon for misappropriation of state funds. The two NSAs have recently deposited another complaint against Ben Ali in France. Those NSAs demonstrate a strong commitment and a high expertise in working on specific cases related to their own country. NSAs based in OECD countries receive little funding from donor agencies compared to developing country-based ones, even though both work for worldwide justice affecting primarily deprived countries. TI national chapters which are based in developing and transition countries, enjoy therefore higher support and funding than their counterparts in Western countries, which are struggling to find financing sources. One could ask whether this is in fact the result of a deliberate choice made by donors who prefer to fund multilateral organisations, better placed in terms of exposure and prominence, to exert pressure internationally and in more diplomatic terms. By having access to international forums such as the OECD, the UN or the G20, the StAR initiative, funded by many bilateral donors, is able to raise important principles in front of the international community and to use the peer pressure mechanism on which such organisations base part of their influencing power. It also has the financial and human resources to publish technical papers on a regular basis.

This does not mean that international initiatives or national NGOs are better equipped for advocacy work. The awareness-raising part of asset recovery agenda undoubtedly needs many efforts coming from various sources, ranging from policy-making proposals at high level in the international community to concrete cases issues to be raised at domestic level by national NGOs. Donors tend however to better sustain the former, and be less supportive of the latter, probably due to conflicting political interests. But national NGOs themselves active in this field usually also prefer to refrain from being financed by donors in order to remain fully independent in a political sensitive topic. The few Swiss NGOs specialized in issues pertaining to the Swiss financial centre (Berne Declaration, Aktion Finanzplatz Schweiz, Alliance Sud) do not receive any funding from the State, except Transparency International Switzerland.

Donors funding the ICAR are well aware that by being well connected to Swiss NSAs and to similar ones abroad dealing with anti-corruption or anti-money laundering issues, the ICAR directly contributes to the prevention and awareness-raising efforts domestically by providing them with scientific and evidence-based research in asset recovery matters. The NGOs which are specialised in advocacy campaigns sometimes lack the technical knowledge in complex legal procedures and investigation of cases, issues which are not easy to capture for somebody without hands-on experience in such matters. The ICAR, by making available accurate and solid information to them helps them better argue and build their cases. Similarly, in order to help the creation of solid empirical information and increasing access to information in Tanzania, SDC started a few years ago to finance the Tanzania Media Fund. This project is dedicated to helping investigative journalism upgrade their skills and disclose corruption cases with solid information in that country. To date, many cases have been exposed by various media.[12] Such efforts are of course only possible in contexts where freedom of expression is guaranteed and, consequently, journalists not threatened.

VI. Returning repatriated assets via civil society organisations

In successful asset recovery cases, Switzerland usually tries to design, in collaboration with the country of origin, the mechanism by which the stolen assets shall be repatriated. The concern of ensuring that the monies return to the people who have been deprived in the first place and are used for the right purposes is at the heart of those repatriation mechanisms. Several solutions have been developed over the years and the cases, with varying degrees of success, involving either an external international agency or NSAs, both implying donor interventions: the Abacha assets have been returned via the WB; the funds have been repatriated to Angola under the fiduciary monitoring role of SDC; the money repatriated to Kazakhstan has been deposited in a purposely created civil society foundation, the Bota Foundation, devoted to financing social programmes.[13] The forthcoming return of the

12 See www.corruptiontracker.or.tz and www.tmf.or.tz.

13 For a review about the restitutions mechanisms for the various cases, read Lugon-Moulin A., 'Asset recovery: concrete challenges for development assistance', in Pieth, M. (ed). *Recovering Stolen Assets*, 2008, p. 303.

Duvalier funds have already started to trigger a large debate launched by Swiss and Haitian NSAs as to whether the monies shall be transferred to and spent by Haitian NSAs or the State itself. One of the reasons why NSAs claim to be the recipients of the repatriated funds is that a return to the State treasury does not offer the guarantee that the monies will be used properly. The few papers available on reviewing how the large sums of money returned to the Philippines' government (Marcos case) and to Peru's government (Montesinos case) have been used demonstrate that this doubt is justified to a large extent: in both cases, the repatriation process did not include an external state of civil society's monitoring role, and the monies seem to have largely vanished in useless expenses.[14]

However, it is not easy to draw general conclusions about the nature of a compulsory external monitoring agency as there are not enough cases to date and the lessons learnt are rather scarce. In fact, the channelling via the WB in the Abacha case did not completely rule out inefficiency in the use of funds.[15] The monitoring, by SDC, of the contracts issued by the Angolan state for buying de-mining material was not a smooth process either and was heavily criticised in the Swiss media. The Kazakhstan story does not prove that it is easier to channel funds via an NSA. The appointment of Kazakh citizens in the board of the Bota Foundation proved to be difficult, and the lack of organisational and implementation capacities of the newly created foundation was a huge challenge, leading to delays and waste of resources (Jimu I., 2009). Those risks are probably inherent to usual difficulties encountered when setting up programmes pertaining to public finance management system.

In the end, NSAs might be best placed to exert an oversight role on those governments' programmes financed by returned assets, with the direct or indirect financial assistance of donors. In Nigeria, the civil society coalition did publish a so-called shadow report, more critical than the official WB and Ministry of Finance of Nigeria re-

14 Jimu I., 'Managing proceeds of asset recovery: the case of Nigeria, Peru, the Philippines, and Kazakhstan', Working Paper Series No 6, Basel Institute on Governance, 2009.

15 Jimu I., ibid. Lugon-Moulin A., ibid.

port.[16] They were also involved in the formal review. The fact that restitution via independent bodies and proper tracking systems is expensive needs also to be taken into consideration when designing repatriation mechanisms.

VII. Conclusion

Asset recovery is a paradoxical topic for donors: on the one hand, it is extremely political because it intersects with national interests, and therefore attracts a lot of attention and visibility, not the least as it reveals the extent to which development assistance worldwide is modest compared to proceeds from corruption emanating from developing countries. On the other hands, asset recovery is a totally marginal topic for development agencies, if measured by the financial volume of assistance specifically earmarked for this anti-corruption subtopic.[17] To sum up the situation at a glance, this assistance is currently limited to funding the following activities: the StAR initiative, the ICAR, a few national NSAs and TI's chapters based in developing countries active in asset recovery campaigns, one-off contributions for solving cases in the form of paying lawyer's fees or domestic actors.[18] One can reasonably estimate this total assistance to be less than USD 50 million annually worldwide. In this picture, the direct collaboration between NSAs and donors agencies accounts for a fair fraction of this already small amount. Why such a discrepancy?

Asset recovery is seen as the end of the chain of the overall topic of corruption, or, even more broadly, governance. It is therefore marginal by nature. Moreover, even though policy coherence becomes

16 World Bank and Ministry of Finance of Nigeria, 'Utilisation of repatriated Abacha loot: results of the field monitoring exercise', 2006.

17 This means excluding funding of wide governance programmes targeted at Justice system reforms or the broader anti-corruption agenda.

18 DfID currently finances two prosecutors in the London Metropolitan Police in an effort to enhance capacities at home in corruption cases affecting developing/transition countries.

more and more important for development assistance, asset recovery remains primarily a domestic issue for law enforcement authorities of concerned countries. As part of the Executive power administration, bilateral donors' agencies are restricted in the way they can collaborate with the Judiciary; they shall not interfere in the handing of domestic cases, except by way of paying lawyer's fees, which is an exceptional solution by nature. Finally, as the issue of asset recovery is so political, donors also face limitations when working on it domestically.

Seen from a pure development perspective, all capacity building efforts face the problem of proving long-term impact. Donors can easily say how many people have been trained, in how many countries, for how long, in what field. However, measuring the long-term results of such training efforts proves to be a headache for many development agencies and across sectors. In asset recovery matters, the ultimate impact of capacity building would be measured by the amounts of stolen monies being returned to their countries of origin. Such measure however raises a number of challenges: how to attribute the merit of a successful asset recovery process only to capacity building? How to trace all cases worldwide so as to obtain a ratio of successful ones against unsuccessful ones? Even though capacity building may always remain a valid tool in development assistance, donors will soon face a problem in proving the impact of trainings in the very complex matters of asset recovery.

For a few years, we have been contemplating a decrease in solved cases, compared to the 1990s' and 2000s'. This translates into less direct donors' interventions in concrete cases, and more emphasis being put on awareness raising efforts at the international level. While such work is certainly needed to help international coherence and standard setting processes, it also bears the risk of diluting the need to work and report very specifically on concrete cases into a more general diplomatic discussion. NSAs, in that landscape, remain with a very important task: their advocacy work is needed both domestically and internationally regarding the pending and the unknown cases, in order to bring them into light in the coming years. The more this advocacy work can be coupled with a part of serious investigation, the more advanced the contribution of NSAs will be in the asset recovery agenda. It is likely that donors might be more interested to build that capacity in developing and transition countries than in their home country.

KEITH OLIVER

'Excellent!' *I cried.* 'Elementary!' *said he.*[1] Mutual legal assistance and the present challenges faced by the legal community in the never-ending quest for the recovery of stolen assets: the victim's options

I. Introduction

With the increase in transnational crime, particularly international financial crime, countries across the globe have become increasingly alive to the imperative of immediate and effective bilateral and multilateral co-operation. This process of co-operation and repatriation has been made more efficient through the use of various international measures seeking to encode and define MLA. This is an on-going battle, and one which has become ever more focused as it is thrust prominently into the global media spotlight. Whilst the merits of MLA and the endeavours made by countries seeking to work together on an international playing field are acknowledged, the flaws with the current system in respect of repatriating stolen assets has become glaringly obvious.

This chapter will seek to address measures which both those in the legal community and beyond can adopt in order to maximise the potential for asset recovery either through the use of MLA or, if necessary, through other alternative means such as international assistance. This chapter is therefore what might be described as a call to litigation arms – a call to the international community to look beyond the narrow focus of MLA as the primary weapon in recovering looted

1 The Adventures of Sherlock Holmes: The Adventure of the Crooked Man (1893) Arthur Conan Boyle.

state assets – and to look at MLA as merely one part of the claimant's armoury in the fight against international financial crime. Real recovery of stolen assets across different continents, time zones, and jurisdictions requires more than state-on-state co-operation with the prosecution and the incarceration of – for example – the corrupt former Minister as the ultimate aim. It requires the contemporaneous pursuit of the wrongdoer in a joined up civil recovery process globally that, if properly co-ordinated and channelled, can secure substantial recoveries – and it can be done on a cost-effective basis. The civil litigation war against the wrongdoer, when combined with an effective media and press strategy, as well as prosecution, can represent an irrepressible pincer movement against the increasingly friendless politician turned potential defendant.

As we shall see, the panoply of civil recovery strategies – from the order that compels the third-party bank or trust company to disclose customer secrets and prohibits, by contempt of court gag, the revealing of that disclosure to the wrongdoer who is their client, through to the nuclear civil search order which is more powerful perhaps than a criminal law search warrant – mean that the tools are available to the practitioner so as to enable civil asset recovery which can be effective, expeditious and highly rewarding for the victim state, agency corporation or individual losers.

Collective and consistent AML laws across the international financial centres and, increasingly, the developing world have contributed to a pariah effect – the increasing rendering of the targeted criminal as toxic to his/her friends, closest associate, and, perhaps most importantly, to his/her professional advisers, trustees and so-called business associates. A zero tolerance parallel sanction approach would lead to more successful prosecutions and greater recovery for the claimants of the looted state funds.

II. MLA and its history

MLA exists in both criminal and civil procedures as a tool for the legal community; although lawyers are, somewhat understandably, likely to be more familiar with MLA in the criminal context since MLA in international crime is certainly more common than asset recovery per se. Securing convictions against those that operate corrupt practices or steal and launder state assets is placed on a higher pedestal than the mere recovery of the assets stolen or laundered by the perpetrators. Such an approach may be flawed by its own self-imposed limits; in the pursuit of the international criminal facing conviction in the criminal sphere, there has to be an effective mechanism for civil asset recovery and the repatriation of stolen assets. While perhaps a widely understood concept, this focus has failed to receive as much attention at the practical claimant focused level. Corruption and other similar crimes need to be addressed with a two-pronged, multiple sanctioned approach involving both criminal and civil procedures acting in tandem in order to make real and contemporaneous progress in righting the wrongs caused by the perpetrators of international financial crime and recovering the proceeds of the misdeeds for the claimant.

Numerous international measures seek to deal with MLA in both the criminal and the civil context. Whilst the various international measures may operate within their respective civil or criminal fields, these are not mutually exclusive concepts despite being part of separate legal processes. Writing from within the UK jurisdiction, there are different authorities who deal with MLA for civil and criminal matters. This is the popular approach taken by the majority of jurisdictions. MLA and the bodies dealing with such requests should be seen as concurrent mechanisms available in the process of asset recovery.

Historically, in the UK, the first statute that attempted to address MLA was the Extradition Act of 1873. The Act allowed for the Secretary of State to require a magistrate or a justice of the peace to require the production of documents or to take evidence for any pending criminal matter in a foreign court as if he/she were taking a deposition in committal proceedings for an indictable offence.[2] The 1873 Act remained in force for just over a century until the criminal law provisions of the Evidence (Proceedings in Other Jurisdictions) Act 1975. The 1975 Act hardly altered the position at all and simply reiterated the 1873 Act by providing for a foreign state to request evidence from either a witness or suspect in documentary form and/or give oral or written testimony. The concept of MLA in civil matters was not addressed at an early stage in the development of MLA and, perhaps more importantly, at this point in English legal history, there was no provision for a foreign state to request UK law enforcement agencies to search and seize material in support of an MLA request.

The slow progress of domestic legislation was thwarted by the catalyst of international agreements, particularly those within Europe. Some credit must lie with the EU for its progressive legislation on MLA in both civil and criminal matters. The starting point for MLA in criminal cases was the 1959 European Convention on Mutual Assistance in Criminal Matters; and it is this particular Convention which has provided the guiding provisions for successive measures, including, but not limited to, the provision that signatory states will provide as wide assistance as possible to requesting states in criminal matters.[3]

One historical hurdle in the context of organised financial crime was the fact that the 1959 Convention also made provision for the requested state to refuse assistance if it considered the offences to be 'political or fiscal in nature or where refusal is made for the purpose of protecting sovereignty, security or public order'.[4] This was clearly a cause for concern. As organised crime increasingly moved across borders, contracting states retained a right to refuse to co-operate and the crucial evidence which was needed to secure a conviction was frequently inaccessible. Consequently, the European Convention was supplemented by the 1978 Additional Protocol to the European Convention signed in Strasbourg. The main purpose of the 1978 Protocol was to remove the right of the state to refuse assistance if it considered

2 Section 5 Extradition Act 1873.

3 Article 1 European Convention on Mutual Assistance in Criminal Matters 1959.

4 ibid, Article 2.

the offence to be fiscal in nature.[5] This development marked the tipping point for legal professionals working in the field of organised financial crime as MLA had become a mechanism through which fiscal offences could be effectively prosecuted in spite of the offences taking place within multiple jurisdictions. The move by those within the EU represents recognition of the fact that, in the laudable desire to secure convictions, there needed to be a cross-border approach to dealing with financial crime.

Comparatively, in the civil context, the early 1954 Hague Convention relating to civil procedure was the starting point for most jurisdictions, with the subsequent Hague Conventions of 1965 on the Service Abroad of Judicial and Extrajudicial Documents in Civil or Commercials Matters and the 1970 Convention on Taking of Evidence Abroad in Civil or Commercial Matters. Similarly to the criminal context, however, it was the EU in 1992 which paved the way for the co-operation of jurisdictions in the civil context. With the Maastricht Treaty signed, the structure of the EU was altered and the three-pillar-structure to policy was introduced. Of particular importance in the context of MLA was the third pillar for 'Justice and Home Affairs' which, among other reasons, was introduced with the aim of enabling close co-operation between member states. There were nine areas of common interest within the third pillar, including international fraud, police and customs and judicial co-operation in both civil and criminal matters. The acknowledgement given by the EU to international fraud is indicative of the sea change in the way in which the member states approached the problem of international financial crime.

The most important aspect of the Maastricht Treaty however, in the context of MLA, was the European focus on 'judicial co-operation in both criminal and civil matters'. Maastricht marked a solid foundation upon which much of the present day MLA within the EU is based. Subsequent Treaties and measures have aimed at strengthening the EU's measures in dealing with organised crime. For example, the Treaty of Amsterdam signed in 1997 focused on the third pillar of the EU and aimed at increased co-operation in the context of, among other things, organised crime. The progressive developments following the

5 *Op.cit*, Note 3.

EC Treaty gave the EU the competence to legislate in the area of private international law. Moreover, Article 65 EC Treaty outlines the EU's aim to improve and simplify cross-border service of judicial and extrajudicial documents, co-operating in taking evidence and the recognition and enforcement of decisions and judgments in commercial cases. It also aims to promote the compatibility of rules so as to address any potential conflict as well as seeking to eliminate obstacles to the 'good functioning' of civil proceedings.

The European approach to MLA in the modern day is founded upon the CoE Convention on Mutual Legal Assistance in Criminal Matters 2000. This convention is the international instrument for regulating the gathering of criminal evidence within European borders. The UK has enacted the Convention through the CICA. The 2003 Act is not limited to Europe, but is applicable to all worldwide requests for MLA. A 2001 Protocol was enacted in addition to the 2000 Convention. The 2001 Protocol dealt primarily with assistance in respect of banking information and confidentiality, with the focal point being crimes such as serious fraud and money laundering. One key provision is the fact that in certain circumstances member states can exchange details of the bank accounts of suspects. Under the domestic legislation in the UK, this is dealt with in sections 32–36 of the CICA.

Outside Europe, in the area of organised financial crime, the US FCPA 1977 has been an effective prototype for subsequent jurisdictions to base their domestic legislation on in order to combat corrupt practices. There was, however, no multijurisdictional approach to MLA with the US until 2003. Prior to this date, there were only bilateral arrangements between member states of the EU and the US. With the signing of the EU/US Convention on Mutual Legal Assistance 2003, a more developed Convention for MLA came into the arena. Contracting states retain the right to refuse a request from the US under any grounds that existed under any bilateral treaty, or if no such treaty existed then a contracting state can refuse on the grounds of security, sovereignty or other essential interest.

It was not until 2003 and the UNCAC that the first anti-corruption treaty was discussed at global level. UNCAC is arguably the most important international measure to date in this area; it is nowadays likely to be the starting point for an MLA request which originates in the context of international financial crime. UNCAC makes it possible to have MLA with any other signatory countries and is the biggest step forward to date on the international playing field as a method through which corruption can be combated in both the civil and criminal spheres.

Article 43 of UNCAC makes it clear that international co-operation in civil matters is still not placed at a par with international co-operation in criminal matters. It states:

> State Parties shall cooperate in criminal matters in accordance with articles 44 to 50 of this Convention. Where appropriate and consistent with their domestic legal system, State Parties shall consider assisting each other in investigations of and proceedings in civil and administrative assets.

UNCAC further states that when considering MLA:

> State parties shall afford one another the widest measure of mutual legal assistance in investigations, prosecutions and judicial proceedings in relation to offences covered by this Convention.[6]

MLA may be requested when 'identifying, freezing and tracing proceeds of crime' and 'in the recovery of assets'.[7] Chapter V of UNCAC provides that the return of assets is a 'fundamental principle'[8] and records the various measures which State parties should take in order to allow for the direct recovery of property, mechanisms for the recovery of property through international co-operation in confiscation and measures for international co-operation in confiscation itself.[9]

Of particular importance to the victims of corruption is Article 57:

> Property confiscated by a State Party pursuant to article 31 or 55 of this Convention shall be disposed of, including by return to its prior legitimate owners, pursuant to paragraph 3 of this article, by that State Party in accordance with the provisions of this Convention and its domestic law.

6 Article 46(1) United Nations Convention against Corruption 2003.
7 ibid, Article 46(3)(k)–(j).
8 ibid, Article 51.
9 ibid, Articles 53– 55.

Article 57 codifies the international process by stating that state parties return the proceeds of embezzlement and the laundering of embezzled assets to their rightful owner, subject to making reductions for reasonable expenses incurred as a result of any investigations conducted by the requested state. In all other offences, Article 57 requires the assets to be returned to the prior legitimate owner if the requesting state can demonstrate that ownership or if the requested state recognises damage to the requesting state.

In addition to UNCAC, the UNTOC also seeks to address international organised crime. Whilst UNTOC is drawn wider than UNCAC in terms of the offences that it governs, international fiscal offences are included within the Convention in Article 6 (money-laundering) and Article 8 (corruption). Of particular reference in the field of asset recovery is Article 12 which states:

> 1. State Parties shall adopt, to the greatest extent possible within their domestic legal systems, such measures as may be necessary to enable confiscation of
>
> Proceeds of crime derived from offences covered by this Convention or property the value of which corresponds to that of such proceeds;
>
> Property, equipment or other instrumentalities used in or destined for use in offences covered by this Convention.

UNTOC provides under Article 13 that a requested state that has received a request from another jurisdiction in relation to an offence covered by UNTOC shall *'to the greatest extent possible'* either submit the request to the competent authorities for the purpose of obtaining an order for confiscation, or submit to the competent authorities with a view to giving effect to an order of confiscation to the extent required. Moreover, following a request, the requested party shall take measures to identify, trace, freeze or seize the proceeds of crime. The concept of dual criminality does however operate, and if an offence is not one within the requested jurisdiction then international co-operation may well be refused.

Article 14 of UNTOC addresses the disposal of confiscated proceeds of crime or property:

> …State Parties shall, to the extent permitted by domestic law and if so requested, give priority consideration to the returning the confiscated proceeds of

> crime or property to the requesting State Party so that it can give compensation to the victims of the crime or return such proceeds of crime or property to their legitimate owners.

And it continues:

> … A State Party may give special consideration to concluding agreements or arrangements on:
> (a) Contributing the value of such proceeds of crime or property or funds derived from the sale of such proceeds of crime or property or a part thereof to the account designated in accordance with article 30, paragraph 2(c), of this Convention and to intergovernmental bodies specialising in the fight against organised crime;
> (b) Sharing with other State Parties, on a regular or case-by-case basis, such proceeds of crime or property, or funds derived from the sale of such proceeds of crime or property, in accordance with its domestic law or administrative procedures.

Under the disposal provisions of UNTOC, state parties are incentivised to engage in international co-operation since agreements can be entered into as to the disposal of any proceeds of crime recovered. Such a provision does not exist under UNCAC, and the provision under UNTOC operates potentially at the expense of the true victims of international financial crimes in spite of the fact that it is the prior legitimate owners who are to be given priority.

Article 18 of UNTOC refers specifically to MLA and includes the much used phrase of 'afford…one another the widest measure of mutual legal assistance' and further provides for the fact that 'mutual legal assistance shall be afforded to the fullest extent possible.' The provision includes methods such as executing searches, seizures and freezing; providing originals or certified copies of relevant documents and records, including bank records; and identifying or tracing proceeds of crime, property, instrumentalities or other things for evidentiary purposes.

The OECD Anti-Bribery Convention is another international treaty which, unlike UNTOC and UNCAC, has a much broader scope as it focuses on the active bribery of foreign public officials in its Article 1(1) (The Offence of Bribery of Foreign Public Officials). With regards to asset recovery, Article 3(3) states:

> Each Party shall take such measures as may be necessary to provide that the bribe and the proceeds of the bribery of a foreign public official, or property the value of which corresponds to that of such proceeds, are subject to seizure and confiscation or that monetary sanctions of comparable effect are applicable.

Furthermore, Recommendation XIII of the Recommendation of the Council for Further Combating Bribery of Foreign Public Officials in International Business Transactions, adopted on 26 November 2009 states:

> ...Member countries, in order to effectively combat bribery of foreign public officials in international business transactions, in conformity with their jurisdictional and other basic legal principles, take the following actions:
>
> i) consult and otherwise co-operate with competent authorities in other countries, and, as appropriate, international and regional law enforcement networks involving Member and non-Member countries, in investigations and other legal proceedings concerning specific cases of such bribery, through such means as the sharing of information spontaneously or upon request, provision of evidence, extradition, and the identification, freezing, seizure, confiscation and recovery of the proceeds of bribery of foreign public officials;

Similar to other treaties, the OECD Anti-Bribery Convention provides under Article 9 that a requested state which has received a request for mutual legal assistance from another in relation to the offence of bribery of a foreign public official 'to the fullest extent possible' provide assistance to criminal investigations and proceedings to the requesting state.

These treaties and international measures, particularly in Europe, have led to increased co-operation across the borders of signatory states. Yet, with only an 'option' to return misappropriated assets to a requesting country, there is nonetheless no guarantee that MLA will secure the physical recovery of assets. This is the problem which legal practitioners currently have to address, as a key element of the process of asset recovery.

Despite the immense growth of AML regimes around the world in recent years, stolen assets can be converted into cash and moved rapidly across multiple jurisdictions in an attempt to avoid recovery. Fortunately, today's practitioner has a wide variety of tools at his/her disposal in order to secure the recovery of monies. Used properly, they can be extremely powerful tools, putting the claimant in a highly advantageous position from the outset.

III. The weaponry of civil recovery

In England and Wales, there are a substantial number of tools which can be used from within the jurisdiction to prevent stolen monies moving at what may well be an alarmingly rapid rate. Perhaps the most potent weapon in the practitioner's arsenal is the proprietary (freezing) injunction. This is available where the claimant contends that the fraudster is holding his/her property, which can include cash, or the traceable proceeds of his/her property (the 'proprietary assets'). Since proprietary injunctions concern a claim over actual property, proprietary injunctions are typically more draconian than a standard non-proprietary freezing order and can restrain any dealings whatsoever in relation to the proprietary assets so that the wrongdoer cannot even use those assets to pay for living or legal expenses. A further advantage, to the claimant, is that the proprietary injunction gives the claimant priority over the wrongdoer's creditors on the asset pool; in contrast to the mere personal rights which are protected by a conventional freezing order.

There will inevitably be times when the claimant cannot rely upon claiming a proprietary right over the wrongdoer's assets and will therefore seek to enforce personal rights. There is a real danger, however, that by the time judgment against the wrongdoer has been secured, he/she will have dissipated his/her assets with the result that there are none left to satisfy the judgment. Such an outcome can be prevented by a freezing order. Unlike proprietary injunctions, freezing orders operate in personam, meaning that they bite on the individual rather than his assets. As such, they do not secure any proprietary rights over the wrongdoer's assets, with the result that the claimant is in a relatively weak position should the wrongdoer become insolvent.

If there are sufficient assets in the jurisdiction to meet the quantum of the claimants claim, then it should be sufficient to use a domestic freezing order confined to the wrongdoer's assets in England and Wales. If, however, the wrongdoer has insufficient assets within the jurisdiction, the court then has the power to grant a worldwide freezing order. It is at this point that bilateral and multilateral treaties between jurisdictions become critical as they, hopefully, will enable the enforcement of such orders. Without enforcement of a worldwide freezing order, it would be no more than a tiger without teeth and thus practitioners need to be live to the international treaties which serve their clients interests and can help prevent dissipation of assets before the issue of repatriation has even been considered.

A freezing order is not the end of the war; it is an interim measure designed to maintain the status quo regarding the assets until the substantial civil claim is determined. The claimant does however have a measure of control in order to prevent the wrongdoer from attempting to circumvent the order by depleting his/her assets improperly through other means; for example, through discharging large bogus debts to third parties. Before any frozen assets are used, however, the wrongdoer may be required by the order to draw first on any surplus assets; in the case of a domestic freezing order, this may include any assets outside of the jurisdiction.

Under the standard freezing order, the wrongdoer is required to give details of the value, location and details of assets within the jurisdiction. For worldwide freezing orders, this extends to elsewhere in accordance with a timetable set out in the order. The claimant may therefore identify the whereabouts of the assets and can notify third parties of the freezing order.

As soon as the claimant suspects that he/she may have been defrauded, it is important that he/she exercises great care not to 'tip off' the wrongdoer, and any of his/her associates, about his/her intention to initiate proceedings, or to take any legal steps to secure assets and/or evidence. Alongside the obvious problem that prior notice may well encourage the dissipation of assets, it may also prevent the court from granting an application for a freezing order on the grounds that to do so would be futile.[10]

10 *Oaktree Financial Services v Higham* [2004] EWHC 2098 Ch. [10].

As a condition of granting the freezing order, the court will require evidence that assets are at risk of being dissipated. In many cases involving financial crime it is more than likely that by the offences very nature, taking fraud as the most obvious example, that there will be allegations of dishonesty against the wrongdoer, and this will be reflected in the evidence in support of the application for the freezing order. The evidence has to reflect rather more than mere statements of concern or unsubstantiated allegations of a belief about the risk of dissipation. Careful consideration must be given in the evidence regarding the wrongdoer's profile and background before the court will approve an application for a freezing order.

Since freezing orders are draconian, the claimant will be required to promise to comply with any order that the court may make in the event that the court decides that the freezing order caused loss to the wrongdoer and, further, that the wrongdoer should be compensated for that loss. The court may further require the claimant to provide some security to fortify the cross-undertaking in damages.

In addition to proprietary injunctions and freezing orders, English law equips the practitioner with a wide range of additional specialised orders which can assist claimants in their fight to recover their funds. For example, the so-called *Norwich Pharmacal* order requires third parties who are mixed up in the wrongdoing, whether innocently or not, to disclose information that will assist in identifying the wrongdoers, allow assets to be traced and to establish the validity of proprietary claims against third parties or tracing assets into the hands of third parties. The most obvious targets for such orders are banks through which stolen funds are believed to have passed. *Norwich Pharmacal* orders extend much further than this however, and they can be made against, amongst others, accountants, solicitors, estate agents, Land Registry, telephone companies and logistics companies.

Similar to the *Norwich Pharmacal* order is the Bankers Trust order. This is only granted in aid of proprietary (tracing) claims. The order provides the means for obtaining disclosure of bank statements and records to show the whereabouts of monies.

Both types of order are usually made without notice, most commonly before the commencement of substantive proceedings. They may both be accompanied by a gagging order which relieves any intermediaries from any contractual obligation to inform its customer, i.e., the wrongdoer, that the order has been made against him/her and that it has disclosed information about him/her. The rationale behind a gagging order is that the wrongdoer will move his/her assets if he/she is tipped off.

There is also the availability of third party freezing orders. These orders, also known as *Chabra* orders, can be obtained against third parties only where there is good reason for believing that assets ostensibly held by them in reality belong to the wrongdoer. They are helpful when the wrongdoer has structured his/her affairs in such a way so as to give the impression that he/she has no interest in the assets in question. They are especially useful when the claimant is confronted by sham trusts or other opaque vehicles which serve to hide the true ownership of assets. The court may hold a discrete trial, if necessary, when there is a dispute as to whether the assets in question belong to the wrongdoer or instead to the third party.

Special disclosure orders can be used against the wrongdoer in order to obtain particular documents that are capable of identifying the nature and location of assets. These may include bank statements that reveal the location of cash assets and identify fund flows.

Section 25 Civil Jurisdiction and Judgments Act 1982 is an invaluable tool. This allows an English court to grant interim relief in aid of proceedings elsewhere, including making domestic and worldwide freezing orders. Foreign proceedings need not yet have been commenced, so long as they will be commenced. The claimant can also obtain an order requiring disclosure of assets to support the freezing order.

Section 25 applications are commonly used when assets are located in England but when the wrongdoer himself/herself is outside the jurisdiction, in the place where substantive proceedings are being conducted. However, section 25 applications may also be helpful when there are no known assets in England, but the defendant is resident within the jurisdiction.

It is vital not only to aim to preserve not only the wrongdoer's assets, but also provide evidence of their wrongdoing. Search orders are an appropriate mechanism as they provide the means for the practitioner to ensure that the wrongdoer does not destroy or suppress evidence if he/she learns of the claimant's intention to take legal action against him/her. The order does not allow forced entry, but only requires the wrongdoer to permit entry. A weakness of a search order, therefore, is that if the wrongdoer fails or refuses to grant access then the claimant must go back to court in order to make an application committing the wrongdoer for contempt. In the meantime, there is a risk that evidence will be destroyed.

Fraud almost invariably involves corporate vehicles. When the wrongdoer has taken steps to deplete assets held by a company improperly, to the detriment of the company's genuine creditors, a further array of tools are available to the practitioner by virtue the Insolvency Act 1986. For example, the court has the power to set aside transactions at an undervalue,[11] making a claim that preference has taken place[12] or claiming that transactions have taken place in order to defraud creditors.[13]

IV. Crossing borders for civil asset recovery and repatriation

In terms of civil asset recovery at a multijurisdictional level, the claimant will be either (1) the requesting state or (2) an identifiable individual or a legal entity which is capable of owning property. If the claimant is a private legal entity, MLA may be cumbersome given its inherent delays and this will prove frustrating for the claimants. As mentioned above, there are however tools which are within the practitioners' arsenal which can, and should, be used and coupled with MLA requests so as to combat the speed and ease which stolen monies can cross borders and, consequentially, jurisdictions.

11 Section 238 Insolvency Act 1986 for companies; section 339 Insolvency Act 1986 for a bankrupt.

12 Section 239 Insolvency Act 1986 for companies; section 340 Insolvency Act 1986 for a bankrupt.

13 Section 423 Insolvency Act 1986.

Practitioners are likely to be more familiar with MLA operating in the criminal sphere. MLA can still be used in the civil sphere, despite there being narrower scope. Foreign states can request that the UK authorities provide assistance for their own domestic criminal investigations pursuant to the provisions of the CICA; and this is also the mechanism through which a criminal case that is based within UK borders will seek to enter into MLA agreements with other jurisdictions.

Chapter 1 of the CICA deals with MLA in criminal matters and sections 1–4 focus upon the service of overseas processes. Chapter 2 deals with the mutual provision of evidence. In particular, section 7 states:

> (1) If it appears to a judicial authority in the United Kingdom on an application made by a person mentioned in subsection (3) –
> (a) that an offence has been committed or that there are reasonable grounds for suspecting that an offence has been committed, and
> (b) that proceedings in respect of the offence have been instituted or that the offence is being investigate, the judicial authority may request assistance under this section.

The CICA continues in sections 8–9 to outline how section 7 requests must be sent, and how any evidence which is obtained through a section 7 request is to be used. Reverting to the tools discussed above, section 10 of CICA governs domestic freezing orders and how following a section 7 request, a domestic freezing order can be made in relation to the evidence in order to protect it whilst it remains in the participating country pending transfer to the UK; whilst sections 11–12 outline the circumstances for sending freezing orders as well as varying/revoking such orders.

An overseas freezing order is governed in sections 20–25 of CICA. Section 22 will give effect to a legally valid overseas freezing order, having made the necessary considerations under section 21, so as to allow a nominated court to issue a warrant in connection with the order allowing for a constable to enter premises, search the premises, and seize and retain any evidence he/she is authorised to search. Section 23 is particularly important, as it allows the nominated court to postpone giving effect to an overseas freezing order in respect of any evidence in order to either avoid prejudicing a criminal investigation which is taking place within the UK or in order to comply with an order which has been made by a court in criminal proceedings in the UK stating that the evidence may not be removed from the UK.

Any jurisdictions who wish to obtain evidence in the UK in relation to criminal matters will need to make a request under section 13 of CICA, and sections 14–15 deal with the powers and nominating of a court in order to obtain the evidence requested. Moreover, under section 16 the ordinary statutory search powers under Part 2 of the PACE are extended to allow for powers of entry, search and seizure if a direction has been given under section 13 or if, it is an application for a warrant or order under section 8 of, or Schedule 1 to, PACE by a constable for the purposes of an investigation by an international joint investigation team of which he/she is a member; and, in accordance with section 16(1) of CICA, the conduct in question constitutes an offence under the law of the requesting state and it would be an indictable offence within England and Wales had it occurred within our borders.

V. MLA – some practical issues

The difficulties of working at a multijurisdictional level combined with a technical and arduous procedure can be a source of great frustration for practitioners working in the field of asset recovery; particularly when the recovery of assets via MLA is a procedure which is not always successful. It must be borne in mind that there is no guarantee that MLA, or any process for that matter, will effectively recover stolen assets. Since MLA can be a slow and cumbersome procedure, unless the requesting state has acted immediately, this potentially leads to problems in respect of assets being dissipated.

MLA requests should contain the identity of the authority making the request; the subject matter and nature of the investigation, prosecution or judicial proceeding to which the request relates; a summary of the relevant facts; a description of the assistance sought and details of any particular procedure that the requesting state party wishes to be followed; the identity, location and nationality of the person concerned if possible; and the purpose for which evidence, information or action is sought.[14] In light of the strict rigid form that MLA requests often take, it is clear how the procedure can be considered cumbersome upon the practitioner. MLA requests require careful and specific drafting directed at meeting the evidential threshold and, critically, the technical requirements of the treaty obligations.

Terminology, let alone language barriers, bedevils the practical application of treaty obligations and, ultimately, recovery. In civil law systems, an action in criminal proceedings against the actual property is referred to as non-conviction based asset recovery. Compare this with common law systems where reference is made to 'civil forfeiture', namely forfeiture, as part of either a conviction based approach or as part of an application under the POCA, or similar legislation in other non-UK jurisdictions.

There is of course a separate, entirely independent problem when seeking to use MLA as a mechanism for asset recovery from those previously discussed. The problem is legal in nature as opposed to procedural: claimants' who find themselves having been defrauded in some manner are no longer the direct legal owners of their property, though they may remain the beneficial owner. Asserting a claim to property which has been subject to forfeiture without legal title will involve complex and costly litigation. There may be no guarantee of a state returning the assets to the individual claimants, despite the call for the claimants to be prioritised in the disposal of confiscated assets.

Hiding assets in other jurisdictions is part and parcel of international financial crime. There are, clearly, significant hurdles in place in the context of civil asset recovery and repatriation. Comprehensive and effective asset recovery requires both foreign restraining orders and forfeiture judgments. This needs to go further than actions stemming from the potential forfeiture following conviction of international crimes; it needs to be possible for foreign restraining orders and forfeiture judgments to be entered specifically against the property in the absence of a conviction in order to support any proceedings for NCB forfeiture.

14 Article 46(15) United Nations Convention against Corruption 2003.

There needs to be recognition of the fact that incentives within the requesting state and the requested state may not be the same; the requesting state has more investment in MLA than the requested state[15]. This problem is reduced by the prospect of sharing in any confiscated proceeds between the two states under an arrangement such as that proposed in UNTOC. Whilst such an arrangement ensures the states adhere to their obligations of reciprocity and allows for the perpetrator to be punished, it may not serve the ultimate problem, namely to enable the claimants to recover their assets and to bring the wrongdoer to criminal justice at the same time. It is, however, arguably a step in the right direction if such arrangements lead to successful MLA requests, enabling asset recovery and repatriation.

In order to effectively ensure that stolen assets are retuned to the victims of international financial crime, state parties need to have legislation in place which gives states the flexibility for forfeited assets to be returned if there is an identifiable victim; pushing article 57(3)(c) UNCAC to its fullest point and ensuring that the claimants at least have a viable possibility of having their assets repatriated to them in the event of a successful MLA request.

It is no secret that General Sani Abacha of Nigeria is suspected to have looted between USD 3 billion to USD 5 billion of public money. When asset recovery proceedings were started in 1999, only USD 1 billion was recovered,[16] showing that claimants' expectations need to be realistic in this complex area of law. In spite of this, it is reported that over a 15-year period, the US, which has the beacon of anti-corrupt practices legislation in the form of the FCPA, recovered over USD 6 billion from cases involving misconduct contributing to the savings-and-loan crisis of the 1980s and 1990s. Given that the legal costs amounted to less than USD 1.5 billion, the United States actually

15 The World Bank and United Nations Office of Drugs and Crime (UNODC), *Stolen Asset Recovery: Global Architecture for Asset Recovery*, http://siteresources.worldbank.org/EXTSARI/Resources/5570284-1257172052492/GlobalArchitectureFinalwithCover.pdf.

16 Nawaz, T (2010) 'Impact of international asset recovery and anti-money laundering efforts on poverty reduction and political accountability' *U4 Expert Answer*, No.230, 17th January 2010, Bergen: CMI/U4.

yielded a 425% return on those cases.[17] This fact, though isolate, does demonstrate that successful and well-thought out asset recovery proceedings can be cost-effective in the long term.

VI. The alternative: civil action

Civil actions under private law are the last avenue for a potential litigant in the event that a criminal prosecution or civil asset recovery is, for some reason or another, not feasible. Whilst previously a rare recourse for those endeavouring to reclaim stolen assets, it is currently gaining popularity in the international sphere, with a number of civil actions being brought against corrupt practices. The inference of course can be drawn that the reason it is gaining popularity and is currently the fashionable route for litigants and practitioners alike is largely due to the failings with the current procedures for asset recovery on the international plane.

Civil action is clearly going to be an attractive option to individuals and legal entities given that they will have a greater deal of control over the case and will also be able to clearly manage the costs of civil proceedings. It allows for asset recovery proceeding independently of the state, and the evidential burden is going to be lower on the balance of probabilities. Moreover, the action is able to focus not only on the wrongdoer but also on associated persons and organisations.

17 Smith, J. Pieth, M and Jorge, G (2007) 'The recovery of stolen assets: A Fundamental Principle of the UN Convention against Corruption' *U4 Brief*, No.2, February 2007, Bergen: CMI/U4.

VII. Conclusion

With increased awareness and increased co-operation between jurisdictions, the collective need for countries to become stronger at fighting international organised crime with a common approach and philosophy is incontrovertible. Rapidly progressing legislation and international treaties in this area are demonstrative of the joined up approach that state parties across the globe are adopting and implementing in order to keep pace with the sophistication of international criminal operations. With MLA, arguably unable, in its present form at least, to provide an effective mechanism for immediate asset recovery and repatriation, the international legal community should, perhaps, be called to arms in order to address adequately the inherent problem of bare information exchange. Critically, the recovery of stolen assets by the weapons of international civil litigation need to be considered as a parallel mechanism in pursuing perpetrators and former dictators who have grossly abused their status and power during their period in office, and secreted stolen state assets overseas.

Civil asset recovery can ensure that stolen assets are correctly identified and located in multiplicity of jurisdictions and returned to their legitimate owners. Corruption and other similar financial crimes can only be tackled with the full force of international contemporaneous measures both civil and criminal. Popular opinion reflects the reality: in order to put the sting into anti-corruption measures, it is the seizure of assets from the wrongdoer or subsequent illegitimate owners and their incarceration that truly reflects an effective system of justice. Ideally, the effective parallel pursuit of the perpetrator – through a combination of civil, criminal and administrative, bilateral or multilateral strategies – community can empower real recovery for the claimant.

The legal community can affect the process and aid the victims of international financial crime, whoever they may be, through employing the measures available to them and ensuring that they truly understand the complexities of litigation at this level. Creativity in responding to challenges to recover assets in other jurisdictions, an understanding of the laws and procedures in different jurisdictions, and the psychology of the culprit and the jurisdictions he/she has employed – particularly those where stolen assets are often hidden – is required. Whilst MLA may be a mechanism through which one seeks to recover assets, it can never be the only effective route to pursue. In fact, since the victims of financial crime may well be someone other than the state itself, the return of assets through the use of MLA is often secondary to the requesting state's attempt to secure information leading to a conviction, assuming that there is such an attempt. Still, how is the claimant to recover stolen assets? Which avenue is most likely to recover assets and is still a cost-effective avenue? These are the most pertinent questions for the practitioner in this field, and the answer is to use every tool that is available, fighting the war against international financial crime from both the civil and criminal angles.

Whether the route chosen is MLA based or, as is recommended here, through a combination of MLA and international civil asset tracing and recovery methods, contemporaneous and consistent media coverage is an integral part of the claimants' weaponry (whether state victim, corporate or individual). International media focus upon the wrongdoer embarrasses and exposes those who would be fiduciaries and other third parties that manage misappropriated assets through a myriad of offshore entities and sham trusts and acts as a significant catalyst to legal recovery through the international courts. Perhaps a global reporting mechanism (for example, an international anti-corruption whistle-blowers hotline could be established and based at IACA in Vienna), would be a useful tool in international co-ordination and sharing of information directed at maximising recoveries for those effected by redolent corruption and global asset theft.

DANIEL THELESKLAF

Conclusions

The *status quo* is pretty clear: Under Chapter V of UNCAC, countries have to take all reasonable measures to trace, freeze and seize proceeds of corruption and assist each other to repatriate such assets. However, billions of monies are still stolen, especially from poor countries, and a certain percentage of these assets are presumably stashed away in new and traditional financial centres. In the last years, only modest amounts of proceeds of foreign corruption have been returned to its rightful owners. So what goes wrong?

Obviously, the traditional approach to combating corruption has shown to be insufficient. A more comprehensive approach to countering this crime, by both prosecuting the criminal offenders and suffocating the financial compensation that arises from such a crime would be a more efficient approach.

The asset recovery processes are complex in nature, requiring not only a change in mind-set but also specialised knowledge from different fields. It also requires the necessary political will from state actors to ensure that the asset recovery processes is effective. This political will may not always be present (or must be generated, as MAX MADER shows in his paper), and the reforms required to ensure an efficient combating of corruption through asset recovery may be seen as unpopular. Here, NSAs play a fundamental role in initiating and supporting such reforms. They work in establishing the necessary critical mass that will in turn drive the necessary political will for change.

The various contributions to this publication show the complexity of the issue. Potential offenders act globally and use all available modern technology to conceal the proceeds of their criminal activity. While a lot has been done to enact relevant pieces of legislation around the globe, in particular legislation to fight money laundering, the level of implementation of those acts remains low. Increasingly, we can witness a vicious circle: The high level of corruption in many countries are an obstacle to the full implementation of anti-corruption legislation and can significantly reduce the effectiveness of institutions that have been set up to fight corruption and recover the proceeds of this criminal activity.

Governments and intergovernmental organisations alone will not be able to resolve this dilemma. If we rely too much on their potential, we will fail. The efforts to trace, locate, seize, confiscate and finally repatriate the proceeds of large scale international corruption requires the support of all potential actors. NSAs in this context include the media, NGOs, the private sector (financial institutions and services vendors such as providers of PEP lists), private donors, the legal community and the academia. The actual recovery will normally be done by the law enforcement agencies of the countries involved. This book is not a call to replace their activities by action of the NSAs. But the latter, as the various articles in this publication show, have specific tools at hand that will support the process of state actors to achieve successful recoveries.

Traditionally, the asset recovery process is dominated by the MLA proceedings. The basis of this instrument dates back to the 19th century where equally strong European powers developed ways how to render each other assistance in criminal matters. It heavily relies on the potential for each jurisdiction to provide for evidence for the existence of a specific crime, its particular elements and its individual authors. This model however does not work between highly sophisticated financial centres and low capacity countries where often the judiciary has been intentionally weakened by the same dictators that are now the opponents of the recovery action. It is more than cynical to demand from a country that has been plundered from a corrupt regime over decades the same requirements than from a jurisdiction that has the financial and human resources to establish highly specialised and professional law enforcement agencies. A lot of work will be needed to reform the MLA process in the future. This necessity is on the table for a long time (for example in the 'Appeal of Geneva', launched by a number of magistrates led by Bernard Bertossa) but too little has been reached yet.

In essence, NSAs remain crucially important to make asset recovery happen in practice. Many of them have collected a large amount of experience in this regard and have been able to focus on those areas where effective progress can be made. This does not go without pushing the boundaries and also risking to failing with a specific approach.

Governments and intergovernmental organisations have for a long time neglected the role of the CSOs in asset recovery. Today, there are a few good examples of successful activities of CSOs in international asset recovery cases. There are of course many more CSOs that are involved in anti-corruption work but only few of them have yet engaged in concrete asset recovery activities. MAUD PERDRIEL-VAISSIÈRE and MAX MADER show such examples how an organisation or even an individual can make a difference and initiate new or support on-going legal proceedings. The role of CSOs can be as multifaceted as these organisations evolve. Their strength lies in their access to media to mobilise public action against impunity and their potential to provide for objective and credible monitoring of returned assets. In the future, modern communication technologies, involving social media, will play an even more important role in the work of these organisations and I would not be surprised if we saw more impact from such activities.

Another role CSOs can undertake, notably in financial centres, is the monitoring of the effectiveness of national anti-corruption and AML laws. TI UK has conducted an excellent review of the UK's AML framework and a large number of European TI chapters are about to publish a set of National Integrity System studies. Organisations such as U4 provide for professional advice and research to guide donors interested in anti-corruption work.

The contribution of the academia is crucial for providing policy makers and international organisations with the relevant scientific background to prepare informed decisions. Academic institutions collect and analyse existing material and draft recommendations for future policies. They can also come up with new, innovative concepts, to tackle the fight against impunity and kleptocracy. MICHAEL LEVI and NICHOLAS LORD show in their contribution that far too little has yet been done to provide for empirical studies that show the nexus between organised crime and corruption. As long as we do not understand these links, we will have difficulties in focussing our activities. The academic output must not alone come from research institutions in the western hemisphere. The situation in the South has to be understood much better: MELVIN AYOGU shows in this paper that the proceeds of corruption should not been seen only as direct proceeds, but should also encompass the indirect damage that corruption causes. This can be seen in hospitals that do not have the necessary equipment to cure patients, in weak institutions, in a non-accountable judiciary, and, in general, in insufficient infrastructure.

The legal community can also contribute to the recovery of proceeds of corruption. While lawyers are often seen as part of the problem – especially when they act as gatekeepers for corrupt politicians and as wilful advisers for multinational companies seeking to provide financial resources to public officials in a innovative' way – KEITH OLIVER and EDWARD H. DAVIS, JR. describe in detail the arsenal of weapons that is available in a common law context to support accountable governments to recover asset stolen by their corrupt predecessors. They also point out how important it is to use civil proceedings as an additional avenue to complement the criminal investigations.

Pecunia non olet said the Romans – 'money does not smell'. The days are gone that the private sector, in particular the financial institutions can be silent over the origin of assets that they accept from their domestic and international clients. Regulators have continuously set up rules to prevent the financial institutions to enter into legal and reputational risks for willingly accepting proceeds of crime, notably stemming from corruption. It will be interesting to see how regulators react to the allegations that major financial institutions in the West and in the Middle East have accumulated large sums owned by the Mubarak and Ben Ali families and their entourages. Some banks even went slightly over the required legal minimum and set up recommendations to prevent the inflow of monies originating from corruption. The Wolfsberg Group of 12 large multinational banks has taken the lead in this.

Traditionally, we think mainly of banks when we associate proceeds of large-scale corruption with the financial system. But this is only one side of the medal. A money launderer, tasked to conceal the origin of a dictator's or his or her cronies' assets does not bother if he lauders the assets through a bank of another financial institution – or even through a non-financial professional or business, e.g. a casino. MARKUS E. SCHULZ describes in his paper how the insurance sector can protect itself against the risks of being involved in such patterns.

The activities of NSAs would hardly be possible without the support of donor organisations. ANNE LUGON-MOULIN, my long-term companion in the leadership of ICAR, describes how donors can support NSAs activities and what the potential outcomes can be. Donors increasingly see the linkages between corruption and lack of effectiveness in the development efforts. A donor that is accountable to its taxpayer can no longer turn a blind eye to corruption and its devastating effects. Supporting anti-corruption efforts by NSAs provides for opportunities to assist development countries in increasing their governance levels on a long-term basis.

Last but not least, there is a need for multi-disciplinary institutions that combines the expertise of many of the facets described above. One important component of such involvement is NSAs contribution to capacity building in asset recovery. Working on popular education and awareness raising, contributing with specific skills and expert knowledge and encouraging communication between states, NSAs complement the asset recovery process in its various stages. The International Centre for Asset Recovery has the mandate and the financial and human resources to support governments, intergovernmental organisations and other NSAs to successfully recover stolen assets. It provides for training, advice on specific cases and a number of practical tools for practitioners.

All NSAs are perfectly placed to come up with new ideas, innovative concepts and proposals on how to push the boundaries. In most governments, officials coming up with innovative approaches are not rewarded. This further increases the gap between law enforcement and a potential offender, as the latter would always seek to improve his or her criminal activities and methods. NSAs have to contribute to reduce this gap. Many of the papers in this book propose new avenues and call on expanding the way we currently think.

In conclusion, NSAs are a fundamental driving force and also assist in filling the gaps in the multi-faceted approach that is required in the asset recovery processes. Whether working with state actors or drawing their attention to perceived gaps, NSAs involvement is crucial. This publication shows the wide variety of possibilities that is open to NSAs to positively influence the success of the processes around asset recovery. Yet, the main responsibility still lies with the individual states, their governments and judiciaries. It has become clear that a combination of the powers and responsibilities of the state, combined with the contributions NSAs can make, will result in the most positive outcomes for the cause of asset recovery. As a result, NSAs involvement should be further developed and encouraged. Curtailing corruption and successfully recovering looted assets profits both the state and the non-state actors.

I am very grateful to all authors to this book and in particular to my colleagues PEDRO GOMES PEREIRA, KODJO ATTISSO, ANJA ROTH and NINA SCHILD, for their invaluable support. My thoughts are with the family of MAX MADER who very sadly and much too young has passed away shortly after having submitted his chapter. His death is a substantial loss to the civil society community in our area. He has set an example how personal efforts can make a difference.

Daniel Thelesklaf
International Centre for Asset Recovery
Basel, September 2011